More Maya Missions

La Quinta del Aserradero

More Maya Missions
EXPLORING COLONIAL CHIAPAS

by
Richard D. Perry
with illustrations by the author

espadaña   press

Also by the author:

Maya Missions (with Rosalind Perry) 1988
Mexico's Fortress Monasteries 1992

To Bob and Ginny Guess

ISBN 0-9620811-2-4
Library of Congress Catalog Card No. 93-072945

Cataloging in publication data:
Mexico —Description and travel
Spanish missions — Mexico — Chiapas
Architecture — Spanish colonial — Mexico — Chiapas

Published by Espadaña Press
PO Box 31067
Santa Barbara, CA 93130

Cover illustration: The church of San Miguel Huistán

CONTENTS

7   Preface

11   Introduction

25   Chapter One
        San Cristóbal de Las Casas
        and the Indian pueblos of
        highland Chiapas

73   Chapter Two
        Comitán and the mission towns
        of southern Chiapas

99   Chapter Three
        Chiapa de Corzo and the missions
        of northwestern Chiapas

118   Illustrations

119   Bibliography

121   Glossary

123   Index

Bartolomé de Las Casas

PREFACE

As this book went to press, an armed rebellion erupted on New Year's Day in Chiapas—the first major insurgency in Mexico for more than twenty years. The rebels were mostly Maya Indians, predominantly landless peasants from rural areas of this troubled southern Mexican state.

Exploitation and ill treatment of the Maya, which dates from colonial times, has continued to the present day. Fanned by difficult economic times and rapid population increase, growing hardship and discontent finally exploded into violence. Although the circumstances of this rebellion are not yet fully known and its consequences unpredictable, within a few short weeks it has already had a profound effect on Mexican life and international public opinion.

The Maya area reaches across southern Mexico, from the Yucatán peninsula to the state of Chiapas, extending southwards into Guatemala and Honduras. These regions have been occupied by the Maya people for thousands of years. The modern Maya still live in the hills and tropical plains of the region, where their ancestors built the enigmatic ancient cities whose ruins attract numerous visitors each year. The Maya region also has a long colonial history, and is rich in the arts and monuments created during the 300 years of the Spanish viceroyalty.

In an earlier volume, *Maya Missions,* we explored for our readers the churches and monasteries of the Yucatán peninsula. *More Maya Missions* deals with Chiapas, adjacent to Yucatán—a scenic land of endless variety, ranging from jagged mountain peaks and cool foggy highlands, to arid savannahs and tropical lowlands.

Spanish colonization was not a happy experience for the Maya people of Chiapas, bringing in its wake dislocation, deadly diseases and harsh exploitation. In many highland communities, against all odds, Mayan languages, customs and folkways have survived the turbulent centuries since the Spanish Conquest, and remain a rich cultural source for ethnographers, historians and travelers.

Although the introduction of Catholicism was a mixed blessing for the Maya, one mitigating factor was the presence of Bartolomé de Las Casas, the Protector of the Indians and briefly the bishop of Chiapas. His humanistic religious and social tenets took root among the 16th century highland Maya and continue to exert their influence today—in controversy—among Indians and clergy alike.

The other positive tangible legacy of Las Casas and his successors is the predominantly religious architecture of colonial Chiapas—the churches and missions built by the Dominicans and others between 1550 and 1820. These historic buildings, both urban and rural, are the subject of this guide. Some are still in daily use while others are abandoned and in ruins, but all merit a visit, not merely for their picturesque and often original architecture, but also for the art treasures they contain and the insight they afford into the unique cultural history of the region.

In preparing this guidebook, I owe many debts. First of all to Bob and Ginny Guess, whose generous hospitality, prodigious local knowledge and cheerful willingness to explore the remote corners of Chiapas were indispensable to the project. My thanks also go to Andrés and Angélica Aubry, who reviewed an early draft of the manuscript and made many valuable suggestions. Sidney Markman's exhaustive study of the colonial monuments of the region has been an essential source, and his encouragement heartening.

Lastly, I should like to pay tribute to my wife Rosalind, who has accompanied me along rough mountain roads and through muddy jungles in quest of abandoned colonial buildings. She has offered much sage editorial advice and been a pillar of support in the production of this guide.

Chiapa de Corzo, The fountain stairway

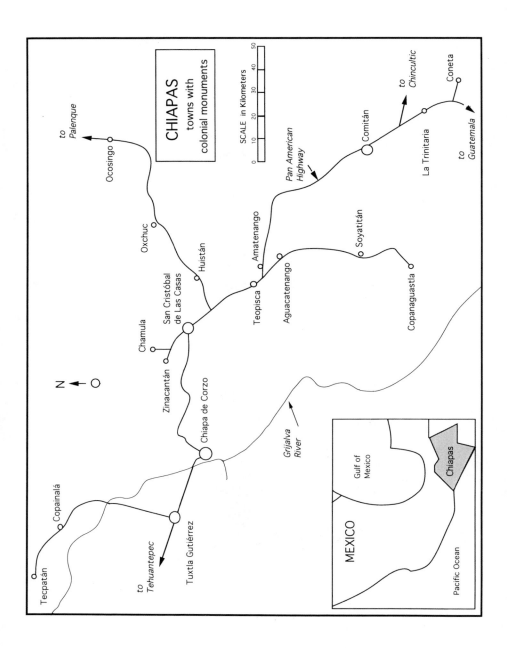

CHIAPAS
towns with
colonial monuments

SCALE in Kilometers

0   10   20   30   40   50

to
Palenque

Ocosingo

Oxchuc

Huistán

San Cristóbal
de Las Casas

Chamula

Zinacantán

N

Chiapa de Corzo

Copainalá

Tecpatán

to
Tehuantepec

Tuxtla Gutiérrez

Grijalva
River

Teopisca

Amatenango

Aguacatenango

Soyatitán

Copanaguastla

Pan American
Highway

Comitán

La Trinitaria

to
Chincultic

Coneta

to
Guatemala

MEXICO

Gulf of
Mexico

Chiapas

Pacific Ocean

INTRODUCTION

Exploring Colonial Chiapas

Chiapas is today the southernmost state of Mexico, but throughout the period of Spanish domination, from 1521 to 1821, it was an impoverished and remote province subject to Guatemala rather than Mexico, then known as New Spain. During that time, the indigenous Maya outnumbered both the Spanish colonists and *ladinos* of mixed race, and exerted a powerful influence on the course of settlement and development there.

Spanish rule necessarily meant the wholesale restructuring of native society and the establishment of a new colonial order. This new order involved radical social, economic and religious changes that are still being felt almost 200 years after independence from Spain.

For the visitor to Chiapas, this heritage is most strongly felt in the presence of its most tangible remnants, the surviving colonial buildings that are the focus of this guide. Aside from a handful of civic structures, including the splendid public fountain in Chiapa de Corzo, these venerable monuments, together with the art treasures they contain, are wholly religious in nature.

Only one truly Spanish town was established in colonial Chiapas, that of Ciudad Real, today known as San Cristóbal de Las Casas in honor of the great Dominican reformer, Bartolomé de Las Casas. And even in this highland city, the Spanish colonial center was surrounded by Indian *barrios*. The handsome baroque cathedral and the urban monastic churches lay within a ring of barrio chapels.

In an effort to convert the large Indian population of Chiapas to Catholicism, Dominican friars launched an intensive evangelization program in the mid-1500s, founding numerous mission towns, or *pueblos de indios,* across the region. Thus many of the early colonial buildings are village churches, which range in importance and scale from major monasteries, like Tecpatán and Copanaguastla, to myriad rural churches and chapels.

Conquest and Colonization

Chiapas boasts a varied scenery with several distinct climatic zones. In colonial times, it was an inland province, smaller than it is today. Known simply as Chiapa, it ranged from the high Sierra Madre on the west, across the tropical Grijalva River valley, or central depression of Chiapas, and up into the cool central highlands to the northeast. The Lacandón rain forest in the eastern lowlands and the narrow coastal strip of the Soconusco to the southwest were administered separately.

When the Spaniards first appeared in the area, the region was a mosaic of ethnic chiefdoms divided by geography and language, torn by warfare and political rivalries, and ripe for conquest by powerful outsiders. Sometime before A.D. 1000, a warlike group known as the Chiapanecs had invaded the region from the north, disrupting trading networks and exacerbating the traditional rivalries between the Zoque people of northern Chiapas and the Mayan communities of the highlands. Only a few decades before the arrival of the Spanish, the Aztecs had penetrated the area from central Mexico, establishing garrisons and exacting tribute from the indigenous peoples, which further strained the political and economic fabric of the region.

Although its inhabitants were declared vassals of the king of Spain as early as 1522, it was not until 1524 that Hernán Cortés, the conqueror of the Aztecs, ordered a military expedition, or *entrada*, into Chiapas. Captain Luis Marín led a force of 30 Spaniards from their settlement of Espíritu Santo on the Gulf of Mexico. This group included Bernal Díaz del Castillo, the veteran warrior and chronicler of the campaign against the Aztecs. The soldiers traveled southwest across the Zoque country and then followed the Grijalva river upstream. Near Ixtapa, they encountered a large force of Chiapanecs but managed to fend them off, at a cost of many casualties to both sides. With the help of local Zoque chieftains opposed to the Chiapanecs, the Spanish boldly counterattacked, seizing the Chiapanec capital of Chiapan and routing its defenders. According to legend, many Indians threw themselves into the nearby Sumidero Canyon rather than surrender.

Other towns in Chiapas quickly submitted. Later the same year, the residents of Chamula, who had suffered the incursions of gold-seeking Spaniards, rebelled. Captain Marín was able to put down the uprising by launching a bloody assault on the Maya settlement from a base camp at Hueyzacatlán, a grassy highland valley that would become the future site of San Cristóbal de Las Casas. For his part in this assault, Bernal Díaz was awarded the town of Chamula in *encomienda*. However, finding themselves surrounded by resentful Indians in a remote area with few resources, the Spaniards did not stay long.

Interest in settling the region was rekindled a few years later. In 1527, a better equipped expedition of 200 Spanish soldiers under the command of Diego de Mazariegos left Mexico City for Chiapas, supported by cavalry, cannon and numerous native troops. The expeditionary force pushed down the Pacific coast, penetrating inland to present-day Tuxtla Gutiérrez. After a brief skirmish they met no further resistance and, once again, most of the Indian towns peacefully accepted Spanish rule. Mazariegos immediately founded a Spanish settlement across the river from Chiapan, which he named Villa Real de Chiapa.

At the same time, Pedro de Alvarado, the conquistador and Captain-General of Guatemala, moved to assert his claim to Chiapas, dispatching a force under the command of his lieutenant, Pedro de Portocarrero. Portocarrero occupied the southern part of Chiapas, which henceforth became known as Los Llanos.

A dispute immediately arose between Mazariegos and Portocarrero over control of the province. In a pre-emptive move, Mazariegos moved his capital up to Hueyzacatlán, the former Spanish base in the highlands, citing its healthier climate and more central location as the reasons for the change. The two rivals met in Huistán and agreed to abide by the decision of the authorities in Mexico City. Alonso de Estrada, the acting Spanish governor of New Spain, decided in favor of his kinsman, Mazariegos, and Portocarrero was persuaded to return to Guatemala. Mazariegos laid out a new Spanish town in Hueyzacatlán, which he renamed Ciudad Real ("Royal City"), taking care to offer building plots and encomiendas to Portocarrero's key lieutenants.

Mazariegos' triumph was shortlived. In the face of a new Indian rebellion the next year—the result of excessive Spanish demands for tribute—he abandoned his new capital, professing illness. A Spanish force, under Juan Enríquez de Guzmán, arrived from Mexico City to quell the uprising, and Mazariegos was put on trial for dereliction of duty. Deprived of his lands and rights by the royal tribunal, he fell truly ill and died the following year.

In 1531, Alvarado, by now the governor of Guatemala, succeeded in detaching Chiapas from New Spain. From 1539 to 1544, Chiapas was governed by his friend, Francisco de Montejo, the *adelantado* of Yucatán. Thereafter, and for the rest of the colonial period, Chiapas was administered from Guatemala. It was divided into two provinces, Soconusco and Chiapa.

Even late in the 16th century, Chiapas remained a backward colonial province, attracting few Spanish settlers. Although some gold was extracted, agriculture and native labor were the principal resources of the province. The colonists exacted tribute from the Indians and exploited the lucrative commerce in *cacao*, the cocoa bean —an important trading commodity in pre-hispanic times. They also established cattle haciendas and planted cotton and sugarcane beside the Grijalva River.

Within a few years, however, European diseases, social dislocation and ill-treatment by the settlers took a heavy toll on the Indians. As the indigenous population declined, demands on the survivors for labor and tribute increased, causing acute distress for the natives and diminishing prospects for the settlers, many of whom left the province. Although there was a slow economic recovery in the late 1600s, it was not until the 18th century that the province showed any measure of prosperity.

Ciudad Real was designated the seat of the Catholic see of Chiapas, initially under the patronage of the Virgin of the Annunciation. In 1531 the city acquired a new patron saint, St. Christopher (San Cristóbal) under whose protection the city lives to this day.

The Spiritual Conquest

Under the papal decree known as *patronato real*, the Spanish kings exercised complete control over the Catholic church in Spain and its newfound colonies, with the power to appoint bishops and send out missionaries. Fatefully, they also created the Spanish Inquisition, to enforce Catholic orthodoxy and root out heresy.

During the earlier reconquest of Spain from the Moors, the monarchs had relied heavily on the religious orders, rather than the established clergy, to convert their new Islamic subjects to Catholicism. The reformed mendicant orders of friars—the Dominicans, the Augustinians and, above all, the Franciscans—proved ideal for this missionary task, committed as they were to poverty, evangelical preaching and teaching by example.

With the fall of the Aztec empire in Mexico, Cortés persuaded the Emperor Charles V that these same dedicated friars should now undertake the conversion of the Indians of New Spain. Cortés knew that the episcopal clergy, long accustomed to the worldly comforts and corruption of the Spanish church, would be unequal to the demands of missionary work in remote regions of the New World. "If these people [the Indians] were to see the affairs of the church and the service of God in the hands of canons or other dignitaries, and saw them indulge in the vices and profanities now common in Spain," Cortés wrote, "it would bring our Faith into much contempt and they would hold it a mockery."

So in 1524, the first Franciscans arrived in Mexico, twelve in number to symbolize the apostolic nature of their mission. The humble friars were respectfully greeted by Cortés and the native nobility, and soon set about their task of converting the Indians and establishing missions. The Dominicans followed two years later and the Augustinians arrived to take up their duties in 1533.

Each of the mendicant orders staked out its own missionary territory: the Franciscans in the valleys of Mexico and Puebla and the Augustinians in surrounding regions to the north and west. The Dominicans extended their ministry southwards, from present-day Morelos into Oaxaca, Chiapas and Guatemala.

Bartolomé de Las Casas

More than any other historical figure, Fray Bartolomé de Las Casas has shaped the centuries-old debate over the nature and consequences of the Spanish dominion of the Americas. As an outspoken defender of the rights of aboriginal peoples, his fiery polemics against Spanish imperial policy and the cruelties of the early conquistadors earned him the title of Protector of the Indians. His lurid account of Spanish atrocities in the pamphlet, *A Brief Account of the Destruction of the Indies*, gave rise to the Black Legend, by which history has often condemned the Spanish Conquest and the excesses of Spanish colonialism that he vigorously protested.

In addition to his controversial historical and public role, he also exerted a less well documented but possibly more enduring influence on the religious beliefs of the Indians of Chiapas. During the few brief years he spent there, with the help of a handful of devoted Dominican missionaries, he schooled the Maya in his own humanistic and egalitarian brand of Catholicism.

Born in 1474 into a wealthy Spanish family, Las Casas studied law at the University of Salamanca. There he was attended by an Indian servant brought back to Spain by his father, who had accompanied Columbus on his second voyage to the New World. Soon after graduating, Las Casas also sailed for the Americas. On his arrival, the idealistic young law graduate witnessed the conquest of Cuba and was outraged by the brutal treatment and enslavement of the natives at the hands of the Spanish settlers. Taking holy orders, he joined the Dominicans and thereafter dedicated his life to improving the lot of the Indians.

Trained as a theologian and legal scholar, Las Casas took the enlightened view that Spanish officials and colonists had no right to exploit Indian labor or society. Even while evangelizing the natives—in his view the sole justification for the Spanish presence in the Americas—there should be no coercion, only peaceful conversion in the apostolic tradition of the early Christian church. In long letters to Emperor Charles V, he castigated the colonists and lobbied for laws to protect the indigenous population from the *encomienda*, the forced labor draft of Indians granted by the monarch to Spanish conquerors. His persistent efforts resulted in the New Laws, promulgated in 1542. Although never fully implemented, this legislation nevertheless set a standard for treatment of the Indians and helped in some cases to relieve their plight.

Las Casas traveled throughout the new colonies of Panama, Nicaragua and Guatemala, excoriating slavers and settlers, and organizing utopian Christian communities of Indians. In 1544, late in his career, he was appointed bishop of Chiapas. His brief sojourn there—two short years—nevertheless became the defining moment in the evangelization of the province. In Chiapas, his missionary efforts among the Indians bore lasting fruit. San Cristóbal de Las Casas, the former colonial capital, today remains the only place in the Americas to commemorate his name.

The Dominicans in Chiapas

Religious conversion of the Maya, although an often proclaimed priority of colonization, was long delayed in Chiapas. A few Mercedarian friars had accompanied the early colonists in the 1530s, but systematic evangelization of the Indians awaited the coming of the Dominicans, led by Las Casas.

Arriving in 1545 at the head of a contingent of friars from the great Spanish Dominican priory of San Esteban de Salamanca, he was preceded by his fiery reputation and was not welcomed by the Spanish settlers of Ciudad Real, who at first refused to let the Dominicans even establish a church in the town.

Bent on defending the beleaguered Indian communities from exploitation by Spanish *encomenderos* and Crown officials alike, Las Casas was determined to implement the New Laws. The friars immediately embarked upon their Spiritual Conquest of the countryside—the peaceful conversion of the Indians to Christianity. Despite their initial difficulties with the colonists, the friars quickly succeeded in evangelizing much of the new province, founding the first missions in the settlements of Zinacantán and Chiapa de Indios.

Accompanying Las Casas was a fellow Salamancan, Fray Tomás de la Torre, who recorded these early Dominican missionary efforts in Chiapas. His account, now lost, became the basis for another history of the province by Antonio de Remesal, the renowned 17th century Dominican chronicler.

Las Casas and his colleagues preached a humanistic form of Catholicism. They taught that as new citizens and faithful Christians, the Indians' principal loyalties were to God, the king of Spain and their own communities, rather than to the colonists. With its promise of autonomy and deliverance from Spanish domination, this liberating brand of Christianity was enthusiastically embraced by the Indians, under the tutelage of the friars. The Spanish settlers, who depended upon native tribute and labor, naturally resisted such radical ideas. After two frustrating years of constant strife, Las Casas was forced to return to Spain in order to plead anew the Indians' cause.

However, with Las Casas out of the way the colonists moved to make peace with the remaining friars, enticing them into Ciudad Real with an offer to build them a church there. The priory of Santo Domingo eventually became the hub of Dominican missionary activities throughout colonial Chiapas.

In 1549, the Crown granted the Dominicans permission to congregate the Indians in a network of rural mission towns, or *pueblos de indios*. During the next decade the friars gathered the Indians from their scattered hamlets into the new settlements, many of which were located near ancestral Mayan villages or sacred sites.

Following the creation of the Dominican religious province of San Vicente de Chiapa y Guatemala in 1551, the pace of construction of churches and residential *conventos* quickened throughout Chiapas. By the 1570s, the Dominican priory of Santo Domingo was completed in Ciudad Real. Substantial priories were also established at Tecpatán, in the Zoque country, and at Chiapa de Indios (now Chiapa de Corzo). Monasteries were also founded in the larger Indian towns of Comitán, Copanaguastla and Ocosingo in the eastern part of the province, each with several dependent *visita* missions.

However, by the late 1500s, the militant idealism of Las Casas had been subverted, as had most of his other utopian ventures. The friars had acquired their own cattle ranches and sugar plantations, all maintained by native labor from the mission towns. They encouraged the formation of Indian *cofradías*, or religious brotherhoods, not only to foster the cults of the saints and the Virgin, but also to provide funds and labor for the friars' varied projects.

As in Oaxaca, the Dominicans enjoyed a missionary monopoly in Chiapas. This allowed them virtually uncontested social, economic and political control in Indian pueblos outside the capital. And in time, the Dominicans forged an alliance with the local settlers and colonial authorities—an alliance that served the Dominicans well during the later colonial period, when outside pressure mounted to replace the friars with episcopal, or secular clergy.

Maya Life and Religion

The Indians fared less well as colonial society developed. The missionaries' success in Christianizing the Maya was less than effective, a shortcoming that the friars often cited to justify their continued presence in the pueblos. As the Maya continued to suffer exploitation at the hands of the Spanish colonists and even the clergy, Indian hopes for earthly salvation faded. Although decimated by disease and deprivation, they never forgot the promise of messianic Christianity as preached by Las Casas and the early friars.

As the Maya clung to their communal religious tradition, with its memories of ancient Maya cosmology and continued to observe the time-honored rites of the agricultural round, they also adopted the cult of the saints and the seasonal rituals of folk Catholicism. Ironically, this syncretic religion was presided over by the same native *cofradías* that had been established by the friars to serve the orthodox Catholic church.

In time, these confraternities came to represent authentic Indian religious life. They served also to maintain some measure of Maya control of their communal destiny and ethnic identity, which were under constant assault from the oppressive Spanish and *ladino* cultures. With its emphasis on penitential rituals, passion dramas and pilgrimages to the shrines of village santos, Maya folk religion functioned almost independently of the official Catholic church, which came to view it as subversive and heretical.

As it developed covertly throughout the Chiapas highlands during the colonial period, this native religion became overt only in the face of great stress and active threats to Indian society and culture. These outbursts took the form of intermittent native revolts, or revitalization movements, and have continued to this day. However, since the Mexican Revolution, the sway of the orthodox Catholic church over the Maya has been relaxed. Although priests still reside in some villages and continue to celebrate the sacraments, the popular religion has followed its own path in many communities, sometimes with the acquiescence of the clergy, especially under the present liberal bishop of Chiapas, Samuel Ruíz García.

During the numerous village festivals, colorful and complex dance-dramas interweave elements from ancient Maya ritual and mythology with traumatic episodes from post-Conquest history. These events have been much studied by anthropologists and become increasingly popular among visitors. But devotion to the traditional religion and the cult of the saints is not universal among the Maya themselves. In recent years, evangelical Christian sects, often led by American missionaries, have gained many adherents among the Chamulas and other villagers, creating conflict and spurring the formation of new splinter communities— yet another painful adaptation of the Maya to social stress and change.

The Colonial Arts and Architecture of Chiapas

The Spanish heritage lives on in Chiapas. In the lifeways, language, culture and religion, customs that were implanted during the colonial period still endure. Colonial traditions are ingrained in settlement patterns, town planning and even the design of new buildings. Each city and pueblo is centered on a plaza dominated by the church—a pattern that is still followed in new towns even today.

Especially in architecture and the arts, time-honored construction materials, techniques and decorative modes that were used in the colonial centuries continue to be employed in city buildings and village plazas throughout the province. Adobe walls, tiled wooden roofs, stuccoed house- and churchfronts, decorative carpentry and ironwork, even the laying out of new buildings and neighborhoods—all are rooted in the natural and human resources of the region as they were shaped during the colonial years.

Colonial Architecture

Because of this persistence of traditional methods and fashions, as well as the frequency of repair and alteration over the years, it is not always easy to ascertain the colonial origin of a monument. In this book, since style may not be a reliable guide to the actual date of a building, documentation of colonial origin as well as appearance has been our guide.

Defining a regional style in art or architecture is a perilous undertaking. Our approach in guiding the visitor has been to focus on the special qualities of each monument. When we admire the elegant brick fountain in Chiapa de Corzo, the ornate stucco facade of Santo Domingo in San Cristóbal, the grand ruined priory of Tecpatán or the magnificent gilded altarpiece in the village church of Teopisca, we know that we are standing before authentic treasures of colonial art and architecture unique to Chiapas.

Most of the surviving colonial monuments in Chiapas are religious buildings, and outside the city of San Cristóbal, most were originally Dominican churches, located in former mission towns. Some, like the churches in Chiapa de Corzo and Comitán, although extensively remodeled over the centuries, are still in use. Some survive in rural villages, again much altered, but still maintained by the Maya as temples for their own religious cults. Others stand in ruins, virtually untouched since they were built centuries ago.

Nearly all the colonial buildings of Chiapas were originally erected between 1560 and 1800, although many were rebuilt in later years. As befitted a poor and peripheral province, costly construction materials and skilled craftsmen were in short supply, especially in the early years. Wood and thatch structures were common. Brick and adobe became the standard materials, even into the late colonial period and beyond. Rough rubblework rather than cut masonry was the rule, especially in rural areas. Even with the introduction of imposing stone facades in the late 17th century, there was a dearth of fine stonecarving; molded and stamped stucco decoration was substituted for more expensive architectural sculpture.

Most churches follow the simplified plan favored by the early Christian church and the medieval Mendicant Orders in Europe: a spacious single nave with a square or polygonal apse to the east and a raised choir at the west end. Naves were usually covered by the wood-beamed and tiled roofs still characteristic of most Chiapas buildings, and were fronted by massive facades capped with arcaded bell gables, or *espadañas*, and side belfries. A squat tower, with an occasional turreted exterior stairway, was part of the ensemble in some larger churches. Cloisters were attached to the principal conventual churches in the city as well as in the pueblos. Although none remain intact today, the convento at Tecpatán and the rebuilt cloister of Santo Domingo in San Cristóbal give some indication of their original appearance.

The early monuments, notably a handful of Dominican monasteries built in the late 1500s and early 1600s, reflect the eclectic Plateresque style which originated in Spain and evolved further in central Mexico. San Esteban de Salamanca—the celebrated Dominican priory which provided the majority of early missionaries coming to Chiapas—is a late example of this style, which emphasized Renaissance detailing applied to fundamentally medieval or *mudéjar* buildings. The style included such elements as stepped Romanesque frames around doors and windows, coffered arches and jambs, the liberal use of corbels and running cornices along naves and around cloisters, and the placement of giant columns, half columns or pilasters in the facade.

The Vernacular Tradition

The more elaborate structures in Chiapas, especially those urban churches built during the late 17th and 18th centuries, mirror the "earthquake Baroque" architecture of Antigua de Guatemala, the colonial capital to the south. This tradition was enriched in San Cristóbal by greater decorative refinement, especially in the use of stucco ornament. By contrast, the majority of rural buildings, notably the numerous mission churches erected during the 1600s and 1700s, fit into a pattern familiar throughout rural southern Mexico, Yucatán and Guatemala.

The use of wood, brick and stucco in the region naturally lent itself to medieval Hispano-Moorish techniques of construction and decoration. The mudéjar tradition, which had developed during the long Islamic occupation of Spain and was perpetuated in the rural churches of Andalusia, also made its way to the New World. This anachronistic structural style persisted in Chiapas into the 1700s and even later—as much a reflection of popular taste as of the poverty and isolation of the province.

It is interesting to compare the colonial churches of Chiapas to those of neighboring Yucatán—the subject of our companion guide, *Maya Missions*.

As in Yucatán, most rural churches in Chiapas started life as primitive missions, often no more than thatched open chapels. Because they used the abundant limestone of the peninsula, more of the early Yucatecan chapels have survived, usually incorporated into later structures. Built of more ephemeral materials like wood and adobe, only sturdier examples have survived in Chiapas, notably those at Teopisca and Oxchuc. Imposing facades, commonly added in the 17th and 18th centuries, are a characteristic feature of churches in both regions. While those in Yucatán generally lack the *retablo* facade format and side belfries typical of Chiapas, their elaborate and imaginative crowning espadañas rarely fail to impress the visitor.

The churches of the Chiapas pueblos are recognizable by their retablo facades, espadañas and diminutive belfries. An innovation inspired by the Counter Reformation, the retablo facade was introduced in the 17th century. It was conceived as a preview of the *retablo*, or altarpiece inside the church and was designed to remind the populace of the authority and doctrinal orthodoxy of the Catholic church and its teachings.

The Retablos

It is in the magnificent church altarpieces that we encounter the finest artistic achievement of the age. Created and assembled by teams of specialized artisans, these retablos represent the high point of the colonial artistic heritage, where the arts of the painter, the sculptor and the gilder come together.

These great retablos were intended to impress. Although structurally conservative—relying for the most part on the classical forms of the early Baroque—they are large, ornate and richly gilded. The detailing is sumptuous, with lavish use of the spiral Solomonic column as well as intricately carved cornices, panels and extravagantly foliated niches. Designed to inspire as well as to instruct the faithful, religious paintings and sculpted images fill the niches, with special emphasis on skillfully carved and painted wooden figures of the saints.

Because many fine altarpieces and most religious sculpture of quality were commissioned for the churches of San Cristóbal, workshops were established there during the 1700s, probably directed by master craftsmen from Guatemala and elsewhere. Although numerous colonial retablos have been lost over the years because of earthquakes, fires or civil strife—not to mention their wholesale replacement by neoclassic altars in the 1800s—the few that have survived in the city and nearby communities afford us some insight into this rich artistic tradition. Outstanding examples are those of the Cathedral, Santo Domingo and San Francisco in San Cristóbal, and the newly-restored main altarpiece at Teopisca.

The colonial buildings and artifacts described in this guide are not merely museum pieces. Although some monuments have been neglected or abandoned, others remain a vital part of community life, still the focus of religious and social traditions unique to this region of the Americas.

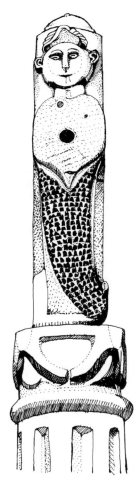

La Sirena, Mermaid relief

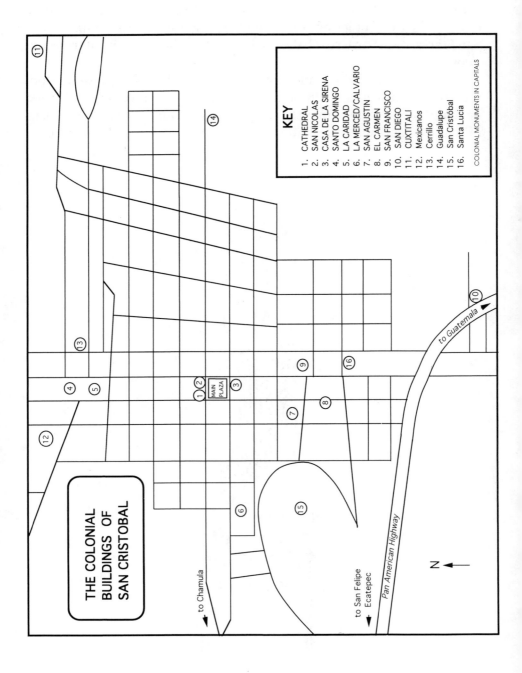

THE COLONIAL BUILDINGS OF SAN CRISTOBAL

KEY

1. CATHEDRAL
2. SAN NICOLAS
3. CASA DE LA SIRENA
4. SANTO DOMINGO
5. LA CARIDAD
6. LA MERCED/CALVARIO
7. SAN AGUSTIN
8. EL CARMEN
9. SAN FRANCISCO
10. SAN DIEGO
11. CUXTITTALI
12. Mexicanos
13. Cerrillo
14. Guadalupe
15. San Cristóbal
16. Santa Lucia

COLONIAL MONUMENTS IN CAPITALS

MAIN PLAZA

to Chamula

to San Felipe Ecatepec

Pan American Highway

to Guatemala

N

CHAPTER ONE

San Cristóbal de Las Casas and the Indian Pueblos of Los Altos

Today, San Cristóbal de Las Casas is still one of the least changed of Mexico's colonial cities. Wandering through the checkerboard of streets and tree-shaded plazas, walking past whitewashed churchfronts with sculpted niches and decorative stuccowork, gazing up at the expanses of tiled roofs resting on overhanging wooden beams, or admiring the rows of pastel-colored houses embellished by wrought iron window screens, the visitor can easily imagine the city as it was in its full florescence in the 18th century.

Los Altos, now as in colonial times, refers to the highland region that surrounds San Cristóbal and extends to its north and east. An early consequence of the Dominican evangelization effort in this area was the founding of numerous *pueblos de indios*, or Indian mission towns. The first of these missions was built at Zinacantán, the most populous native settlement in the area at the time of the Spanish Conquest. Although this mission subsequently burned down and was replaced by a post-colonial structure, colonial churches have survived in other highland Maya villages, notably at Chamula, Huistán and Oxchuc.

San Cristóbal de Las Casas

"The city of Chiapa Real (San Cristóbal) is one of the meanest cities in all America... In this city there is no parish church, but only the cathedral, which is mother to all the inhabitants. Besides, there are two cloisters, one of Dominicans, and the other of Franciscans, and a poor cloister of nuns, which are burdensome enough to that city."

Thomas Gage (1625)

Thomas Gage's timing was poor. The English Dominican friar arrived in San Cristóbal in 1625, when famine and disease had taken a fearful toll of the Indians and the residents of the city found themselves in straitened circumstances. The early optimism of the 16th century colony had faded, and an economic depression had taken hold. It was not until the end of the 17th century that the city would recover its strength and embark on the great building program that has given the city its present appearance.

Founded in 1528 by a small group of Spaniards led by the conquistador Diego de Mazariegos, the colonial city of Ciudad Real, the "Royal City" was among the first to be established in the New World. Transplanted to the highlands from the earlier lowland settlement of Villa Real de Chiapa, the new capital was located in the Jovel Valley, a lush, well watered basin overlooked by volcanic peaks known in ancient times as Hueyzacatlán.

Ciudad Real was laid out on a grid, one of the earliest examples of that novel town plan in the Americas. The city was also unique in its provision for both Spaniards and Indians to live side by side. The 16th century town center, located around the main plaza, was called El Recinto and was reserved for the tiny community of Spanish colonists and their families. The surrounding residential areas, collectively known as Los Barrios, were settled by the various native groups that had accompanied the Spaniards to Chiapas: Tlaxcalans and Mexicanos from central Mexico, Mixtecs from Oaxaca and Quiché Maya from Guatemala. Although the colonial city was unfortified—another New World innovation—the barrios provided a buffer against an outside attack, which may have been the main reason for their inclusion in the urban plan. Two encircling rivers and the surrounding water meadows also gave the city some measure of protection, despite the constant threat of flooding.

The Spaniards were served by the parish church, later raised to the status of a cathedral, while each of the native quarters had its own *ermita*, or barrio chapel. This dual character of the city, Spanish and Indian, established during colonial era, persists to this day. In fact, the recent rapid growth of outlying Indian barrios have tipped the demographic scales in the favor of the Maya.

Ciudad Real served as the principal Spanish town of the province throughout the colonial period, under the authority of the Audiencia of Guatemala. In 1824, however, Chiapas was annexed by the newly independent Mexico, and in 1892 the regional capital was moved to the lowland town of Tuxtla Gutiérrez, closer to the Pacific coast.

Cut off from rapid change and modernization during most of this century, San Cristóbal has thus been able to preserve more of its original character than most other colonial Mexican cities—a source of great pride for *coletos*, as the citizens of San Cristóbal like to call themselves.

The Colonial Buildings of San Cristóbal

In San Cristóbal and the surrounding communities we can trace the changing styles of colonial art and architecture as they developed during the viceregal era: a few 16th and early 17th century religious and civil buildings, predominantly mudéjar or Plateresque in style; the fine baroque facades of the late 1600s and early 1700s; and the blossoming of the city churches and convents during the 18th century.

We start our exploration of San Cristóbal in the main plaza, known as the Parque Central. The **Cathedral** and adjacent church of **San Nicolás** stand on the north side, while on the south side we find **La Casa de la Sirena**, a former conquistador's palace now converted into a hotel.

Next we describe the churches of the various religious orders, which are dotted about the city. First, the magnificent Dominican monastery of **Santo Domingo**, north of the plaza, and its neighbor, the church of **La Caridad**. Then we visit the remarkable nuns' church and convent of **El Carmen**, situated southwest of the Parque Central. In this same quarter we also find the churches of **La Merced**, **San Agustín** and the well preserved conventual church of **San Francisco**.

Then we turn to the barrio churches of the colonial city: **El Calvario**, a small chapel located behind La Merced, **Cuxtitali**, a barrio with its colonial chapel and bridge on the northeastern edge, and the little chapel of **San Diego** on the southern fringes. Lastly, we visit the Franciscan mission town of **San Felipe Ecatepec**, west of the city, and the tiny 18th century chapel of **La Quinta**, located on a former bishop's estate in the hills to the east of San Cristóbal.

San Cristóbal, The Cathedral

THE CATHEDRAL

The cathedral that Bartolomé de Las Casas knew during his brief tenure as bishop of Chiapas, between 1545 and 1547, was not the imposing masonry building we see today. Founded in 1528 as the Spaniards' parish church and dedicated to Our Lady of the Annunciation, the church was given cathedral status ten years later when the see of Chiapas was created, by royal order.

The primitive cathedral was a flawed adobe structure, its walls cracked by earthquakes and its rude foundations eroded by the floods that plagued the colonial city. Amazingly, through the repeated patchings, shorings up and additions, the 16th century fabric of the building survived until the late 1670s, when it became clear that the cathedral was in danger of collapse. Over the next 20 years it was almost entirely reconstructed in a heavy baroque style, using Antigua Cathedral in Guatemala as a model but retaining the original basilican plan of nave and side aisles.

Essentially, this is the building we see today, although work continued during the 1700s, the early 1800s and into the present century. Further remodeling followed a major earthquake in 1902, when the interior arcades were rebuilt in the fashionable neoclassical style. Recent renovations, including restoration of the superb altarpieces, have brought the cathedral to its present excellent state of preservation.

The cathedral still occupies its original site. The long, heavily buttressed nave, distinguished by the pedimented doorway and florid neoclassical windows, almost fills the north side of the main plaza. The apse and episcopal archive lie at the east end, with the little church of San Nicolás tucked in behind them at the end of the block.

The West Front

The cathedral faces a narrow forecourt, currently being extended into a spacious plaza that promises to greatly enhance the westerly prospect of the magnificent facade. Despite the addition of arcading around the doorways, the cathedral facade has preserved its ornate, late 17th century character.

The broad retablo facade consists of two main tiers, surmounted by an extravagant baroque pediment of sinuous profile punctuated by obelisks and ball-topped finials. On the lower tier, paired Tuscan columns enclosing pedimented sculpture niches divide the wide central bay from the narrower lateral bays. Giant projecting arches, added to provide seismic protection, frame each of the three doorways and enclose lunettes above.

The upper tier has a richer texture, highlighted by the decorative stuccowork that is a hallmark of several San Cristóbal facades. Ionic columns separate the ornamental openings, niches, heraldic medallions and relief sculptures. All these architectural elements are set against a luxuriant tapestry of geometrical shapes, intricate arabesques and foliated motifs, variously carved, stamped, molded, incised, burnished and painted. The complex play of shadow, shape and color on the facade, especially in the slanting light of the early afternoon sun, is a visual feast not to be missed.

Facade Iconography

Nuñez de la Vega was a Dominican bishop of San Cristóbal in the late 1600s. An energetic and ambitious prelate, he was largely responsible for the new urban look created during this era, notably in the baroque facades of the cathedral, of Santo Domingo and of San Agustín.

In his 1696 scheme for the cathedral facade, Nuñez, a stern champion of Catholic orthodoxy and the church militant, signaled a return to the evangelistic fervor of the spiritual conquest—but without its previous humanistic face. For example, instead of showing St. Christopher—the peaceable patron of the city—the central relief above the choir window depicts Santiago Matamoros (St. James the Moorkiller), the warrior saint so beloved of the conquistadors.

In the same vein, the militant Archangel Michael (San Miguel), celebrated for vanquishing the forces of darkness, appears prominently on the upper tier of the facade, flanked by the Four Evangelists representing biblical authority. For extra emphasis, San Miguel appears again in the lunette above the north entry.

The Virgin of the Apocalypse (La Purísima) stands in the lunette above the central doorway, flanked by St. Peter and St. Paul—the pillars of the early church—installed in elaborate niches. Above them we find St. Dominic (left) and St. Francis, both noted preachers and the founders of mendicant orders. St. Paul, the traditional advocate of Church authority, reappears on the upper tier (left), above a relief of the Virgin of the Assumption. On the other side, above the Risen Christ, a haloed Moses points magisterially to the Commandments. By these symbols, the cathedral front glorifies the reinvigorated church of the Counter Reformation, seemingly intolerant of any but Catholic orthodoxy—an unequivocal message directed to Indian and Spanish residents of the city alike.

The Altarpieces

Early in the present century, the architect Carlos Flores added the Corinthian colonnades which divide the main nave from the side aisles. Rows of correctly classical columns with fluted white shafts stand in vivid contrast to the dark wooden ceiling. The broad, well-lit east end provides an ideal setting for the principal treasures of the cathedral—its

The Cathedral, Statue of San José

three large gilded altarpieces. The central retablo of Los Reyes (the Three Kings)—a theme depicted in the main altarpiece of many Mexican cathedrals—is transitional in style. It combines the Solomonic column characteristic of the 17th century with the *estípite* pilaster associated with the late Mexican baroque or Churrigueresque style, a motif seldom encountered in Chiapas. A statue of St. Christopher, the patron saint of the city since 1539, stands in an upper niche—his only appearance in the cathedral.

However, it is the two accompanying altarpieces that command our special interest. Both of them—San José (St. Joseph) on the south aisle, and El Perdón (dedicated to Our Lady of Forgiveness) on the north side—are believed to have been brought here from the nearby Jesuit church of San Agustín. They were companion pieces to the exquisite main retablo of that church, which is now installed in San Agustín Teopisca, a pueblo south of San Cristóbal (see Chapter Two). This pair of rare gilded works may be modeled on the famous retablos of Antigua Cathedral, which were destroyed during Guatemala's devastating earthquake of 1773.

Both altarpieces are tall, elegant and conservatively classical in form, although their surfaces scintillate with sumptuous ornament of great refinement. Richly encrusted spiral columns and panels of exquisite arabesque relief frame the paintings and sculptures on the two main tiers and crowning pediment. Sharply projecting cornices separate the tiers, some carved with scrolled profiles and others hung with delicate bell pendants.

The altarpiece of San José is the finer of the two. A noble statue of the youthful saint, holding the infant Jesus, occupies the central niche on the first tier. A second, more accessible, statue of the saint—the object of great popular devotion—stands on a pedestal beside the retablo. Although both are of 18th century origin, the freestanding image is particularly expressive. The saint's curling hair and beard and his pale, melancholy features in the Guatemalan style contrast with his ornate coronet and flowing brocaded robe with opulent *estofado* texture—a sublime example of Spanish colonial figure sculpture.

San Nicolás

SAN NICOLAS

This elegant temple, now partly obscured by a high wall, occupies the northeast corner of the main square, behind the cathedral. Originally, the little church was known as San Nicolás de los Morenos, and served a congregation of blacks and mulattoes.

Founded as a hermitage between 1615 and 1621 by Juan de Zapata Sandoval, an Augustinian bishop of Chiapas, the first building was located slightly to the north of its present site. When the episcopal palace was enlarged late in the 1600s by the ambitious Bishop Nuñez de la Vega, the chapel was rebuilt to face the plaza and continued to serve the burgeoning black population of the colonial city.

Today, viewed through its high arched gateway, the little adobe chapel looks much as it did in 1700. The temple-like facade, simply but harmoniously proportioned, reputedly was the model for numerous other small mission churches built throughout highland Chiapas. The large rounded doorway is flanked by paired half columns enclosing slender sculpture niches. A lofty espadaña, set between unusual cylindrical corner turrets with conical roofs, surmounts the facade.

Recently, the cornices and triangular pediments have been picked out in brash reds and browns against the white stucco, imparting a festive appearance to the facade. The niches remain empty, as they have always been. Although encouragement of the public cult of the saints was the principal reason for the introduction of the retablo facade into colonial church architecture, funds for the statuary at San Nicolás never materialized.

Elongated arched windows with stepped frames handsomely accent the nave and sanctuary block. The octagonal hipped roof of the square sanctuary rises well above the level of the nave, supported upon corner squinches. The chapel and adjacent sacristy bear the typical tiled roofs of the region, their overhanging eaves supported by wooden rafters with exposed *zapatas,* or carved beam-ends. A picturesque exterior stairway leads up to the wooden choir loft.

Currently being restored as a museum of diocesan history and religious art, the spare but pleasing lines of the chapel interior can now be seen to particular advantage. The insignia of the colonial *cofradía* of La Encarnación is painted on the plank ceiling and emblazoned on the sanctuary arch.

When completed, the museum is expected to display some of the treasures of the cathedral archive, including priceless historical documents and a unique sequence of bishops' portraits from Bartolomé de Las Casas to the present day.

La Casa de la Sirena

LA CASA DE LA SIRENA

Opposite San Nicolás on the other side of the Parque Central stands La Casa de la Sirena, now the Hotel Santa Clara. With the exception of the Casa de Mazariegos in the southwest corner of the plaza, which has been virtually rebuilt, it enjoys the distinction of being the only non-religious 16th century building to survive in San Cristóbal.

So-called because of the primitive relief of a mermaid (*sirena*) mounted on its northeast corner, La Casa de la Sirena was the residence of Andrés de la Tovilla, an early conquistador of Chiapas and encomendero of Copanaguastla (see Chapter Two). It was probably built in the mid to late 1500s. Although much smaller in scale and poorer in design and execution, the facade is distantly related to the magnificent Casa de Montejo in Mérida, Yucatán—perhaps not by chance, since Francisco de Montejo, conqueror of Yucatán, was Captain-General here in the 1540s. Despite alterations over the centuries, the somewhat battered facade of carved stone and stucco, applied to an underlying brick fabric, has remained largely intact.

The decorative entry porch has an authentic folk-Plateresque character, with predominantly medieval elements imposed on a classical, rusticated background. Emblazoned above the rectangular doorway is the archaic heraldic device of a knight's visored helmet, covered with a turban and flanked by spreading laurel leaves. Freestanding candelabra columns with grooved shafts and crude basket capitals frame the entry, capped by finials that project in front of the overhead cornice. Naive, frog-like felines with open jaws and high looped tails crouch on swagged capitals atop the finials. Rosettes decorate the base of each finial and continue along the frieze that runs beneath the cornice.

Twin reliefs of seahorses face each other on either side of the overhead window, balanced atop what appear to be segmented calabashes. Fanciful baluster colonettes frame these quaint reliefs, which are crowned by rainbow-shaped arcs—also studded with tiny rosettes.

A second decorative window, further along the facade towards the plaza, is framed by a squared *alfiz* molding of mudéjar ancestry, supported on lions-head brackets. Sinuous reliefs of wide-eyed, winged sirens with long, seductive tails, wearing exotic feather headdresses adorned with tendrils, undulate on either side of the window. The crude sculpture of a man in Indian costume, a much later addition, is mounted on the southern end of the building.

CHURCHES OF THE RELIGIOUS ORDERS

Aside from the cathedral and San Nicolás, almost all of the major churches in the city were founded and built by the various religious orders, whose members outnumbered the diocesan clergy throughout the colonial era. As a group, these churches are the heart of the colonial architectural heritage of San Cristóbal.

The grand Dominican priory of **Santo Domingo** is the most important of the conventual foundations. Its close neighbor, the church of **La Caridad**, belonged to a hospital run by the Order of St. John. The church of **La Merced** was founded by the Mercedarians, the first of the religious orders to arrive in the city. The church and convent of **El Carmen** were built for the Carmelite nuns, just around the corner from the Franciscan monastery church of **San Francisco**. The church of **San Agustín** was not founded by the Augustinians, as might be expected, but by the Jesuits, who also established the first college in Chiapas.

SANTO DOMINGO

In 1546, the Spanish *vecinos* of Ciudad Real had second thoughts about their hostile reception of the Dominicans a year earlier. Extending the olive branch, they offered the friars land for a monastery and promised the labor of several thousand Indians to build it. After the uncompromising Bishop Las Casas left for Spain in 1547, the Dominicans came to an understanding with the townspeople, and soon work started on the monastery, which was sited on a dry hillside north of El Recinto.

The foundation stone of this first Dominican priory in Chiapas was laid by the bishop of Guatemala, Francisco Marroquín. By royal order construction of the monastery was expedited so that by 1551, a modest wood and adobe church with a convento had been erected on the site under the supervision of Fray Pedro de la Cruz. Following a crippling lightning strike in 1563, the church was rebuilt and completed by the 1580s. The present fabric of the church, however, dates largely from the 17th century—the product of an ambitious rebuilding program that culminated in the magnificent facade we see today.

Approached by a steep western stairway, the church is bounded by a raised forecourt and walled atrium. From the atrium, the church presents an almost military appearance, its nave braced by buttresses capped with formidable merlons. Above the crossing rises a prominent segmented

Santo Domingo de San Cristóbal

MUSEO

38

dome, girded at the corners by four sentry box belfries that also bristle with merlons. Spiral colonettes mounted on pillow pilasters frame the crenelated south doorway—a distinctive feature apparently derived from the church of La Merced in Antigua, Guatemala.

The West Front

The present churchfront dates from the late 1600s and is among the most ornate baroque facades in Mexico. Although influenced by the screen-like Oaxacan facades of La Merced and La Soledad, the profusion of sculptural detail and rich surface ornament gives the Santo Domingo facade its own special grandeur—originally enhanced by glowing colors.

The facade rises through three broad tiers crowned by an elaborate baroque pediment flanked by octagonal belltowers. Each tier is divided into three main bays by paired columns. These are formed of ornate shafts with contrasting spiral bands, headed by Tuscan and folk Ionic capitals. The columns are set one in front of the other, magnifying the impression of depth and movement conveyed by the exuberant surrounding decoration. Ornamental curvetted and scrolled pediments animate the facade, capping every opening and niche. Sinuous mermaids recline in the volutes bracing the pediment, which is surmounted with sharp obelisks.

The Santo Domingo facade eclipses all others in the region in sumptuous surface texture. Its decorative vocabulary of religious images is woven into a rich stone and stucco tapestry of geometric patterns, filigree and foliated arabesques.

Reading the Facade

As with the cathedral, the iconography of the Santo Domingo facade was determined by Bishop Nuñez de la Vega, the advocate of a resurgent church militant and a strong Dominican presence in Chiapas.

The retablo facade glorifies the roles of the saints and the Dominican order in the triumph of Catholicism in the New World. In the spirit of the Counter Reformation, statuary and religious symbols emphasize the traditions of religious orthodoxy as well as the evangelistic heritage of the Order of Preachers.

St. Hyacinth of Poland (San Jacinto) and St. Peter Martyr, important Dominican saints revered as apostles to distant lands, occupy the niches flanking the central doorway. Ornamental Christic monograms are carved into the plaques above the two figures, and tiny narrative reliefs suggesting the biblical story of Daniel in the lions' den are cut into the entablature overhead, to emphasize the power of faith. More mermaids or sirens decorate the jambs of the doorway, and the grotesque mask and figures above suggest a medieval or antique origin, evoking the apocalyptic imagery of the early years of the Spiritual Conquest.

Flanking the choir window, reliefs of the radiant Holy Sacrament, attended by censer-swinging angels, symbolize the central mystery of Christianity. St. Thomas Aquinas, a staunch defender of Catholic orthodoxy, stands to the right of the window, while on the left is the mutilated statue of St. Vincent Ferrer, the fiery Dominican preacher in whose honor the Dominican province of San Vicente de Chiapas was named.

The squat figure of St. Dominic, the Spanish founder of the order, occupies the central niche above the choir window. The saint bears the traditional star upon his forehead and a rosary around his neck. On either side of him, two-headed Hapsburg eagles—symbols of royal patronage and authority—imperiously spread their wings. The saint is accompanied by two Dominican nuns: on his left, St. Catherine of Siena, and on the right, St. Rose of Lima, the first saint of the Americas.

In the niche above him, another Catherine, St. Catherine of Alexandria, poses with her wheel. This saint held special significance for the Dominicans of San Cristóbal, for it was on her feast day in 1546 that the friars and their Indian converts joined their Spanish neighbors in a mass of reconciliation. The Dominican emblems of the foliated cross of Alcantara framed by a rosary are emblazoned on the crowning pediment, flanked by more angels.

The Interior

The decorative treatment of the Santo Domingo nave is unique in the Americas. In harmony with the ornate surfaces of the facade, both sides are sheathed with gilded relief panels. Along this golden avenue unfolds a luminous sequence of carved and painted side retablos interleaved with original colonial paintings.

A typical section, opposite the south door, incorporates the pedimented retablo of El Niño Atocha—a shimmering structure resplendent with Solomonic columns. Here are painted panels in "eared" and oval frames, and the bell-shaped pendants characteristic of many altarpieces in the region—all enfolded in a swirling mass of golden foliage.

The extravagant rococo pulpit and stairway, lavishly carved with gilded panels of interwoven grapevines, enhance the richness of the interior. A lofty dome opens up above the crossing, supported on pendentives painted with portraits of four Dominican popes: Pius V, Innocent IV and two Benedicts, XI and XIII.

The south transept was extended to accommodate the Rosary chapel, a common adjunct to Dominican churches. More fine ornamental carving graces the gilded retablos around the chapel. The main altarpiece, dedicated to the Virgin of the Rosary, was created in the same opulent vein as the nave retablos, its carved religious images and paintings framed by intricately worked spiral columns adorned with grapevines.

The two 18th century side retablos dramatize the Passion of Christ in large paintings and sculptures. The center relief of the altarpiece on the west wall is an unusual portrayal of the Trinity, in which a bearded God the Father (El Padre Eterno) cradles the body of Christ in the style of a Pietá.

The Convento

The former convento of Santo Domingo has been completely rebuilt and refurbished as the Museo de Los Altos, an excellent regional history museum of the Chiapas highlands. The museum boasts an informative permanent exhibit with local examples of colonial artesanry, fine silverwork, including the massive bishop's throne, and an equestrian figure of Santiago Matamoros—a spirited processional folk sculpture.

From the reconstructed cloister, the visitor enjoys an excellent view of the dome of the church, with its turreted corner belfries, and the reverse side of the facade pediment, which is decorated with stucco reliefs not visible from the front.

The convento also houses a weaving cooperative that promotes the sale of textiles and other colorful crafts from Mayan villages around San Cristóbal.

Statue of Santiago (Los Altos Museum)

LA CARIDAD

In May 1712, the miraculous image of an Indian Virgin Mary appeared in the Maya village of Cancuc. The religious authorities refused to recognize the cult and persecuted its leaders, sparking a nativist revolt that threatened to drive the Spaniards from the Chiapas highlands.

Massacres of Spaniards and ladinos began in outlying towns. As the insurgent Indians approached the gates of Ciudad Real, the frightened residents hastily summoned troops from Guatemala and Tabasco.

By November, the superior Spanish forces had brutally put down the rebellion. The ladinos credited Our Lady of Charity (La Caridad) for their salvation and celebrated by parading her image through the streets. In gratitude, Bishop Alvarez de Toledo vowed to erect a church and charity hospital in her honor.

Dominican lands beside Santo Domingo were purchased by the bishop, and an existing barrio chapel was demolished in order to build the new hospital. The hospitallers of St. John, known as *juaninos*, were chosen to operate the hospital, which included a chapel and convento and was dedicated to San Juan de Dios. Of this complex only the cloister patio survives, now much remodeled as a shopping precinct.

The church of La Caridad was constructed between 1714 and 1716, beside a generous tree-shaded plaza known as La Alameda. With its retablo facade and prominent domes, the church looks much like a smaller Santo Domingo.

Although it lacks the sculptural richness of its grander neighbor, the facade—reputed to be the work of Diego de Porres, an eminent architect from Antigua, Guatemala—is still impressive. Its verticality is accentuated by projecting pilasters, some with curved profiles, that create a powerful chiaroscuro effect in the brilliant highland sunlight. The espadaña and flanking belfries, studded with sharp merlons, soar high above the tiled roof of the nave.

Inside, the wood-ceilinged nave gives way at the east end to a spacious, sunny sanctuary, home to a luxuriantly gilded altarpiece whose clustered spiral columns radiate warmth and light beneath the blue-toned dome. The figure of Our Lady of Charity stands conspicuously on a pedestal in the center niche of the retablo. Locally known as La Generala—a rank and title bestowed on her by the grateful citizens—she wields her staff of office and wears the military sash of a Spanish general.

The large elevated chapel on the north side of the church has an interesting history. Originally it was the shrine of El Señor del Sótano (Christ of the Dungeon)—a secret cult that had grown up among the neighboring barrio dwellers dispossessed of their former place of worship. With permission from a later bishop, however, an officially sanctioned chapel was raised on the site, funded by alms collected in the city barrios and surrounding Indian villages.

This otherwise undistinguished chapel features a handsome baroque doorway on its west side. Although it cannot be seen from the street, the

La Caridad

doorway may be viewed from an interior patio. The chapel does contain a few colonial sculptures of interest, notably a robust pair of Roman soldiers beside the crucifix on the main altar, and a dashing late baroque image of San Martín—still the object of great devotion from Indian worshippers. The mounted figure of Santiago Matamoros that formerly stood in the chapel has been removed and now rests in the nearby Museo de Los Altos.

Walking around the outside of the church, the visitor may admire the two domes of the church: a high cupola above the sanctuary block, adorned with undulating ribs and a decorative lantern, and a lower dome over the chapel, guarded by eroded crocodile gargoyles crouched on the four corner buttresses. The church precincts are usually crowded with Maya selling their colorful handcrafts.

EL CARMEN

On March 23, 1993, a disastrous fire struck the church of El Carmen. It burned the roof and engulfed the newly restored interior, totally destroying its priceless contents and colonial furnishings—a tragic loss for San Cristóbal and us all. This rambling former nunnery, south of the main plaza, is surrounded by a burgeoning cultural center—an attractive complex of old and new buildings occupying the conventual precincts.

The 17th century church tower, a landmark known to locals simply as El Arco, is at the heart of the project, which also encompasses the church, the adjacent Carmen Chapel and plaza. An annex to the colonial convento, La Casona, has been converted into the Casa de Cultura. An oval auditorium and a convention center have been added. The tower was restored in the 1970s and, beginning in the 1980s, the church was the focus of a program of renewal that included restoration of the wooden roofs and, most recently, the choir.

Once located on the fringes of the colonial city and formerly occupied by the 16th century chapel of San Sebastián, the site was acquired in 1610 for the elite Conceptionist Order of nuns. There they founded their convent of La Encarnación—the name by which it was known until the present century. Dependent upon donations for their construction, both church and convento rose slowly. The tower was built after 1677 and the Carmen Chapel, on the north side of the church, was not added until 1764.

El Carmen, The tower

The nuns' church is characteristically plain. Its only exterior feature of note is the folk-baroque north portal, a design of outsized *estípite* pilasters and floral scrolls applied in the style of Antigua. The primitive relief of an eagle with wings outspread stands above the doorway, accompanied by lions rampant enclosed in heart-shaped medallions.

The portal of the adjacent Carmen Chapel is somewhat more elaborate, although still provincial in style. Its triple-tiered retablo form is partitioned by fluted and spiral columns with petal capitals and surmounted by a spreading espadaña with baroque flourishes. Above the doorway, the weathered wooden statue of a headless saint rests in a niche emblazoned with the Carmelite insignia.

The Interior

Before the fire, handsomely crafted artesonado ceilings roofed both church and chapel. The chapel of Nuestra Señora del Carmen, especially, was a gem among San Cristóbal interiors. Carved openwork beams spanned the room, beneath a red and gold plank ceiling. Burnished wall panels, incised with foliated designs to emulate gilded retablos, were suspended from the ceiling like tapestries, enveloping the windows and the doorway. The altarpiece of the Virgin displayed a colonial sculpture of St. Anne and the Virgin, whose figures were rendered in popular Guatemalan manner, with pallid features and richly-textured flowing gowns.

The main church was less inviting, its unadorned walls and white neoclassical altarpieces radiating little warmth or charm. A few colonial sculptures were to be found there, including the kneeling figure of St. Nicholas of Tolentino, a prominent Augustinian saint. A stoic San Sebastián stood on the main altarpiece, another early sculpture that may have belonged to the first chapel on this site—a particularly sad loss. Also lost was a large 18th century group portrait of the Carmelite sisters.

The Tower

Only the monumental tower escaped the holocaust. This unique structure formerly served as a city gate as well as the church belfry. When first built, the tower spanned the main thoroughfare into the colonial city. The nuns were required to incorporate an arched gateway and grant a public right-of-way that was in force until quite recently. Although the church contained its own narrow, raised choir (now burned), a second choir may have been part of the tower, since multi-level or double choirs were a common feature of colonial nuns' churches. Commonly found in southern Spain, such multiple use towers are a rarity in Mexico.

Stylistically, this intriguing tower reveals many classic mudéjar features. Giant arched niches on the north, south and east sides encase all three stories of the tower, with corner columns on the upper level forming an alfiz above each arch. Although the north side has been altered—remodeled after one of the periodic floods or earthquakes that have afflicted the city—the southern face has retained its 17th century design virtually intact. Classic Hispano-Moorish accents include corbelled brick moldings and decorative star-and-lozenge stuccowork. An upper belfry, crowned by a segmented brick dome, is partly hidden behind a parapet.

The most remarkable detail, however, is the miraculously preserved wooden ceiling spanning the interior of the gateway. A decorative carved star, with a pendant rosette at its center, covers the apex of this classic eight-sided vault. In an effort to protect this fragile work, metal gates now bar the entry.

SAN FRANCISCO

Because of the Dominican monopoly in the countryside, the Franciscans, their chief rivals, were confined to evangelizing the Indian barrios around the city. In 1575, the Bishop of Chiapas invited the Franciscans to establish a friary in Ciudad Real, on a tract of marshy land to the south of El Recinto. By 1580, four friars from the Franciscan province of the Holy Name of Jesus, in Guatemala, were living there in a rude adobe-and-thatch mission.

This primitive building was replaced by a permanent monastery in the 17th century and rebuilt again early in the 18th century. Compared with the sumptuous Dominican priory of Santo Domingo across the city, it was a modest structure, in keeping with the humble traditions of the Order of Friars Minor.

Although the convento and cloister have since been demolished, the church still stands, facing a small plaza—all that remains of its once spacious atrium. Under the trees in the atrium stands a colonial stone baptismal font, its shell basin carved with stylized floral reliefs.

The salmon and white facade is articulated in a spare provincial style with plain cornices and pilasters springing from stylized, pot-shaped bases. A few later embellishments, including the swagged and serrated friezes below the cornices and the sawtooth arch above the choir window,

San Francisco

date from the mid-18th century. The curvetted pediment and squat belfries, sprouting urn-shaped finials, may also date from this time.

This cool classical church exterior hardly prepares the visitor for the mellow interior, with its rich baroque furnishings. Handsome fretted wooden beams and a painted plank ceiling span the freshly renovated nave, which harbors a wealth of golden altarpieces and colonial artworks.

Spread beneath the high hipped roof of the sanctuary is an ornate 18th century altarpiece, the largest in Chiapas. The retablo has a scalloped outline in the Guatemalan style, and is lavishly gilded with rococo arabesques and flourishes. Its numerous compartments, framed by knotted cords, house a cycle of oval canvases illustrating the exemplary lives of St. Francis and St. Clare, the founders of the Franciscan First and Second Orders. Several smaller retablos complement the main altarpiece along the nave, and in the large side chapel, a fine pedimented retablo, elegantly framed by gilded Solomonic columns and reminiscent of those we saw at Santo Domingo, contains naive paintings of the Nativity.

SAN AGUSTIN

In 1767, at the height of their influence, the Jesuits were summarily expelled from the New World. Suddenly, this proud religious order, which for generations had nurtured the colonial elite in its schools and colleges, was forced to depart, leaving a yawning cultural and educational void. For in Chiapas, as elsewhere, the urban churches and colleges of the order were virtually the only centers of higher learning. But depart the Jesuit fathers did, leaving the Mercedarian Bishop Vital de Moctezuma to pick up the pieces and divide the spoils from their abandoned buildings.

The fortress-like church of San Agustín lies two blocks south of the main plaza, attached to the University of Chiapas Law School. Both church and convento were once part of the Jesuit college erected here between 1695 and 1708. The stripped church interior is now used as an auditorium. The adjacent law school occupies the site of the former convento and seminary, whose remodeled neoclassical arcades continue to grace the central courtyard.

San Agustín

Set back from the street behind a vestpocket park, the battered west front has lost its upper gable and belfries. Fortunately, it still preserves sections of decorative stuccowork, including stamped rustication similar to that found on the cathedral facade. Carved above the choir window is an unusual relief of three pear-shaped hearts. The device in the center is the Jesuit symbol of the Sacred Heart, to which the church was apparently originally dedicated. The flanking hearts are thought to represent, on the right, the pierced heart of the Virgin of Sorrows, and on the left, the episcopal device of Bishop Nuñez de la Vega. This energetic 18th century prelate, the sponsor of new facades for the cathedral and Santo Domingo, was also the force behind the establishment of the Jesuit church and seminary. According to tradition, his heart is interred before the main altar.

The best preserved architectural feature of the church is its south porch, bracketed between two of the sturdy buttresses that brace the long nave. Cone-capped, fluted Doric half columns flank this arched entry, which boasts a handsome pair of colonial-style paneled doors. An arcade of three niches, framed by a sawtooth frieze, separates the doorway from an elaborately framed upper window, which is surmounted by monograms of Christ.

Another unusual entry porch is recessed into the rear of the apse, a square block raised above the level of the nave at the east end of the church. Superimposed on the rounded doorframe is a polygonal archway, surmounted with flattened merlons and once again, the IHS monogram of Christ.

Following the expulsion of the Jesuits, the church continued to serve for a while as a seminary chapel. But with its progressive deterioration, culminating in the partial collapse of the roof in 1880, the surviving retablos and church furnishings were gradually dispersed.

San Agustín was justly famous in the 18th century for its superb set of baroque altarpieces, although none of them now remain in the church. Amounting to fourteen in total, their creation inaugurated and sustained the tradition of fabricating high quality retablos in the colonial city.

Some have been destroyed or dismantled, but a fortunate few have been preserved in other locations. The magnificent main altarpiece was saved and transported to Teopisca, where it still stands in the newly renovated parish church (see Chapter Two). The two splendid retablos of El Perdón and San José in the cathedral were moved there from San Agustín in the late 1700s. Another may be among those installed in Santo Domingo.

LA MERCED

Mercedarian friars came here with the conquistadors and ministered principally to the Spanish residents of colonial Ciudad Real, rather than to the Indians of the barrios. The old Mercedarian monastery, located just outside El Recinto, west of the main plaza, was the first to be established in the city.

Faced by a long, elevated forecourt, the imposing church of La Merced was almost entirely rebuilt early in the present century, from its colonnaded "wedding-cake" front to its brittle neoclassical interior. The only surviving colonial remnant is the 18th century sacristy, whose archways and massive supporting pillar are decorated in colorful folk-art style.

Sprouting from the rampant lions at its base, rising tendrils of painted foliage entwine the pillar. On the underside of the arches, bands of classically-inspired grotesque ornament, incorporating sirens and stylized masks with fan-like feather headdresses, curve upwards to meet bas-reliefs of the sun and moon. An inscription, dated 1757, is incorporated in the floral frieze above the arch, and in the spandrels, the Hapsburg imperial eagle almost disappears in a profusion of foliage and flowers.

The Maya presence in the city churches remains pervasive. At almost any hour within their precincts, one may encounter Indian families, sometimes accompanied by professional rezadores, *seated on the floor praying and chanting before an altar. Wreathed in smoke and copal incense, their faces illuminated by flickering candles, these little groups remind the visitor of the continuing vitality of Maya life and customs in San Cristóbal and Chiapas.*

THE BARRIO CHAPELS OF SAN CRISTOBAL

Throughout colonial times, the Spanish residents of the colonial center of Ciudad Real were outnumbered by the Indians of the surrounding barrios, who had settled here from many different parts of Mexico and Guatemala.

Mexicans and Tlaxcalans from central Mexico, many of them auxiliaries who had accompanied the conquistadors, lived in adjoining barrios on the north side. Mixtecs and Zapotecs from Oaxaca resided in San Antonio and San Diego to the south of the plaza. Quiché Maya from Guatemala established themselves in the outer barrio of Cuxtitali, while freed slaves from Chamula and Zinacantán gravitated to the neighborhood of El Cerrillo, near Santo Domingo. The Franciscan order ministered to many of these native communities, founding several of their barrio churches, or *ermitas*, as they were known.

Despite the growth of the city, most of these barrios have retained their individuality, although not their original ethnic identity. All have their distinctive ermitas, some of them humble like the little chapel of San Antonio, and others quite elaborate as, for example, the engaging church of Mexicanos.

Only a few of the remaining chapels, however, are authentic colonial buildings. These are the ones we focus on, although these too have been altered a great deal over the centuries.

The Cuxtitali bridge

EL CALVARIO

Hidden away in a shady courtyard behind La Merced is the neglected little church of El Calvario. These days, it is in poor repair, its walls cracking and its roofbeams rotting away. Although the present structure dates from the 18th century, little is known of its history. At one time it belonged to the Franciscans and may have served as an *ermita* for the Indians of the western barrios.

El Calvario is a modest building, similar in form to other barrio chapels of San Cristóbal and to some rural mission churches of Chiapas. The boxy nave is fronted by a brick and stucco retablo facade, whose simple lines are traced by plain ribbon pilasters and molded cornices, accented in peeling reddish-brown paint. Small blank side niches echo the large rounded arch of the doorway and bands of arabesque relief border the octagonal window above. An attractive espadaña surmounts the facade, flanked by volutes and small side belfries topped by pyramidal merlons. A representation of the Calvary cross, emblazoned with the instruments of the Passion, is placed at the apex of the gable.

The image of Christ on the cross is prominently displayed on the white and gold folk retablo inside the church. He is flanked by the thieves, Dismas and Gestas, his companions in crucifixion, shown lifesize. A few late colonial paintings line the nave, including a frayed but minutely detailed Christ of Redemption, in muted reds and blues. Christ sags from the cross, bleeding profusely, in a stormy landscape with the hill of Calvary in the background. Two angels kneel to collect His precious blood in a chalice while God the Father and the Holy Spirit look down from heaven with compassion. The stricken Mary, portrayed here as the Virgin of Sorrows, bows her head in grief.

Cuxtitali

CUXTITALI

This charming little ermita church is located at the heart of a barrio on the northeast edge of the city. Built in the 1650s, it was originally subject to the nearby priory of Santo Domingo.

Cuxtitali is a classic pueblo-de-indios church, its simple nave covered by a pitched artesonado roof in the Chiapanec style. Brick buttresses reinforce the original adobe walls and an external stairway on the north side gives access to the raised, wooden choir.

The facade is a rustic delight. Recently, its naive architectural and decorative elements were picked out in baby blue against the brilliant whitewashed front. The rounded arches of the various openings—the doorway, the choir window, the side niches and the upper bell arcade—create a pleasing counterpoint to the grid of flat pilasters and string courses. Whimsical corner volutes and a zig-zag frieze energize the undulating gable of the espadaña, which is also accented by a trio of red bells.

But the most intriguing feature of the facade is the cluster of naive stucco reliefs depicting the instruments of Christ's Passion. The sacred heart, embossed above the choir window, stands amid the scourge, the crown of thorns, the crowing cock and the hammer and nails, accompanied by a pair of hovering angels. A ladder and an overflowing chalice appear on the adjacent pilasters flanked by a folksy sun and moon, reminiscent of the reliefs at La Merced.

Seasonal decoration of the church reaches its height during the barrio fiesta of El Dulce Nombre de Jesús, held early in January. At that time, the venerable statue of San Sebastián, which stands on an altar in the church, is dressed in an elaborately looped loincloth, Guatemalan style, in readiness for his saint's day at the end of the month.

The Cuxtitali Bridge

A picturesque covered bridge, known locally as the Peje de Oro, spans the Rio Amarillo just beside the *periférico*, or ring road around San Cristóbal. Apparently unique in Mexico, this isolated wooden bridge is almost certainly of colonial origin and once marked the traditional eastern route into the city.

Anchored by stone abutments, it is protected by a tiled roof supported on wooden posts and four stout corner piers, lending it the unlikely appearance of an oriental pavilion. Located on the fringes of Cuxtitali, the bridge has recently been restored and is now open to foot traffic.

San Diego

SAN DIEGO

Now divided by the Pan American highway, the former Zapotec barrio of San Diego has lost much of its colonial character. The modest Franciscan church is severed from the rest of the neighborhood and faces directly on the highway, perilously exposed to the wear and tear of this busy artery.

But behind its bare little plaza, currently a sooty rendezvous for Indian charcoal sellers, the freshly painted chapel is spick-and-span. Across its whitewashed front, giant pilasters alternate with blank niches—painted blue to create a bold, almost abstract pattern. Ornamental scrolls, finials, swags and diaperwork on the curving gable and side belfries are also outlined in blue, adding a bright, folk-art touch to the facade.

The rest of the chapel is very much in the regional mold. Its adobe nave, covered by a tiled roof with broad eaves, terminates in a fortress-like stone apse. Like the west front, the windows along the nave are accented in dark blue—a treatment also accorded to the little bandstand in the plaza.

An elaborately dressed image of San Diego, the Spanish Franciscan saint, adorns a modern altar in the nave. Alongside it hang several old canvases depicting archangels, no doubt survivors from a colonial retablo long since dismantled.

SAN FELIPE ECATEPEC

Located beside a sharp curve in the Pan American highway, this rustic mission town clings to the sheltering slopes of a wooded valley just west of San Cristóbal. Now virtually a barrio of the expanding city, it was a separate village in the colonial period.

In 1625, Thomas Gage received a rousing welcome here. "The whole village of St. Philip waited for us, both men and women, some presenting us nosegays . . . others dancing before us all along the street, which was strewn with herbs and orange leaves and adorned with many arches hung with garlands for us to ride under until we came to the church."

One of the first missions to be founded by the Dominican order, about 1550, San Felipe was later ceded to the Franciscans. The primitive adobe church was greatly expanded in the 1600s, when masonry buttresses strengthened the nave and tiles replaced the old thatched roof. During the same period, the narrow rubblestone sanctuary was added and the formidable stone facade erected. The plain exterior, with its mix of

San Felipe Ecatepec

materials and uneven finish, proclaims the humble origins of the church, and the detailing of the facade and windows reinforces the feeling of an authentic pueblo-de-indios mission.

Viewed from the walled forecourt, the west front is especially impressive. The facade rises in three tiers, culminating in a wide arcaded espadaña that towers above the nave behind.

Elevated at the head of a steep flight of stone steps, the west porch dominates the main tier. Two massive wall buttresses, inset with niches, anchor the simple arched doorway like a medieval gateway. Flat pilasters, crudely incised with fluting and diaperwork, divide the two upper tiers and enclose a low, Romanesque-style choir window and two larger side niches. Roughly formed baroque volutes bracket the crowning espadaña, which is flanked by slender belfries with high, round domes that add even greater height to the facade.

Inside the church, a broad plank ceiling with wooden tie beams spans the nave, abutting at the east end a triumphal sanctuary arch inset with niches. Beyond the archway lies the narrow squared apse, covered by an angular hipped roof.

Several intriguing colonial furnishings enliven the rural simplicity of the spacious church interior. A large gilded altarpiece in provincial *estípite* style, dedicated to El Señor de Esquipulas—a popular Guatemalan santo, occupies the sanctuary. And two pairs of smaller baroque retablos face each other across the nave. Other curiosities include a gaily painted wooden confessional and the monumental carved stone baptismal font placed just inside the entrance.

Before leaving San Cristóbal, we should mention some of the notable post-colonial city churches. These include the church of Mexicanos, a neo-Gothic fantasy by the celebrated coleto architect, Carlos Flores, which was erected in 1904 on the site of the old colonial barrio chapel and which still contains a pair of 18th century retablos. The church of El Cerrillo, located just behind Santo Domingo in the heart of the 16th century barrio of the same name, was entirely reconstructed in 1890. The colonial chapel of San Antonio, rebuilt in 1887 according to a facade inscription, remains buried in a tiny barrio beside the highway on the southwest side of the city.

Standing in its own plaza south of the Parque Central, the attractive temple of Santa Lucia, although of colonial origin, was completely refashioned in neoclassical style by the architect Nicolás Figueroa in the late 1800s and has been fully restored in recent times. The tiny hilltop chapel of San Cristóbal, a shrine to the patron saint of the city—much venerated by muleteers in earlier times and now a favorite of local taxi drivers—was an 18th century hermitage and family chapel. It too was rebuilt in the mid-1800s and restored in the 1940s. The other hilltop church of Guadalupe, across town on the east side, dates from the 19th century.

La Quinta

LA QUINTA

Hidden away in a bucolic valley of red soil and green banks surrounded by pineclad hills, the delightful little creekside chapel of La Quinta is all that remains of an 18th century bishops' country retreat. The chapel is perched above the ruins of a 19th century sawmill—now abandoned.

The episcopal hacienda was established here in the 1760s by the colorful Mercedarian bishop, Vital de Moctezuma, who claimed descent from the Aztec emperors. His successor, Bishop Vargas y Rivera, a native of Peru and also a Mercedarian, undertook the construction and decoration of the chapel. The chapel faces west and, because of its steeply sloping site, appears most imposing from below. Diminutive twin towers anchor the elevated facade, flanking a recessed porch spanned by a lobed mudéjar arch. The towers are linked on the upper level by an exterior wooden gallery, which the visitor can reach by squeezing up a narrow spiral stairway that winds up inside one of the towers. The gallery is protected by its own pitched, tile roof—a feature rare in Mexico but common in New Mexico and rural South America.

Aside from its setting and dollhouse-like charm, it is the richly-textured west front that gives the chapel its special character. The towers are surfaced with stucco relief reminiscent of the cathedral and San Agustín in San Cristóbal, roughly rusticated along the base and then covered by stamped, incised plaques higher up. The belfries are encrusted with a profusion of blue and white rosettes, curving palm fronds and half shells like lemon wedges, and are capped by rounded domes with baroque finials and merlons on each corner, embossed with crosses.

A rustic folk altar, dedicated to San Martín, almost fills the tiny chapel interior. Two of the baroque churchyard gateways still stand, one nestled beside the chapel and the other isolated below on a grassy slope dotted with black sheep.

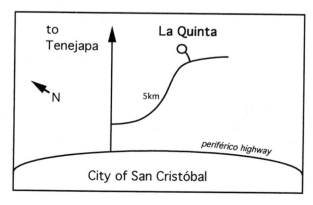

THE INDIAN PUEBLOS OF LOS ALTOS

The highland communities surrounding San Cristóbal are home to numerous Maya Indians. Long studied by anthropologists, linguists and folklorists, these living descendants of the ancient Maya still speak their ancestral languages, wear traditional clothing and observe their unique religious and social customs. Most of the Maya live in hamlets known as *parajes*. These are commonly located on the periphery of the main village centers, which are regarded as sacred places primarily devoted to religious ceremonial.

Starting in the 16th century, the Dominicans established missions in the largest of the highland Maya villages. **Zinacantán** was the first mission town to be founded in Chiapas. Its primitive thatched church burned down after a few years and was replaced by permanent stone buildings in the 1600s. The present imposing church, however, is almost entirely post-colonial and is of interest primarily for its folk santos and the communal Maya festivals that take place in its precincts throughout the year.

Some colonial buildings have survived, although considerably altered over time. These include the churches at **Chamula**, the well known Maya town north of the city, and those at **Huistán** and **Oxchuc**, both located to the east of San Cristóbal and in late colonial times subject to the Dominican monastery at **Ocosingo**.

SAN JUAN CHAMULA

The celebrated church of San Juan Chamula, the dominant structure in Chamula center and traditional focus of religious life there, was originally a Dominican building. Although remodeled over the centuries, it remains one of the few pueblo-de-indios churches to survive in a form close to its 16th century appearance.

The first mission was founded here during the Spanish Conquest. Following the failure of the Chamula rebellion in 1524, at least three Maya communities were resettled in the new village, which formed part of an encomienda granted to the famous chronicler and conquistador, Bernal Díaz del Castillo. In 1549, the Dominicans built a primitive chapel here, which was supplanted by a stone church towards the end of the 16th century. As it was visited by a priest from Santo Domingo, no convento was ever added.

Chamula is nestled in a highland valley northwest of San Cristóbal and reached via a narrow road that winds up through wooded hills. Three green-painted tree crosses mark the village entrance, from where the visitor can view the ruined church of **San Sebastián**, standing in the middle of the village cemetery. Simpler in form but clearly related to the main church of San Juan, this abandoned chapel is thought to occupy the site of the first mission at Chamula.

In addition to the large, open plaza, the imposing church of San Juan has its own walled forecourt, or atrium, with three arched entrances. Today, as in colonial times, this is the arena for the vivid religious processions and ceremonies that crowd the Chamulan ritual calendar. During these celebrations, the church banners and santos are paraded around the atrium, which reverberates with the explosions of gunpowder and the blare of brass bands.

In plan and construction, San Juan Chamula exemplifies the rural missions of Chiapas. Nave walls of coarse stone are braced by buttresses and pierced by slender windows with stepped frames. A pitched terracotta tile roof covers the church.

The west front is especially striking, with its broad arched doorway, balconied choir window and lofty espadaña towering above the village. The portal dominates the facade, its great coffered doorframe recalling the classic Dominican Renaissance doorways of Coixtlahuaca and Tlaxiaco, in Oaxaca. Alternating button and rosette reliefs around the doorway are

San Juan Chamula, from San Sebastián

picked out in red and blue-green, adding a colorful folk touch. Narrow sculpture niches, now empty of images, are set one above the other in pairs beside the doorway.

The enormous choir window breaks dramatically through the cornice above the doorway into the gable overhead. The prominence of this window is puzzling, although the presence of a balcony in front suggests that it may have been used originally as a preaching pulpit, or even an elevated open chapel. A narrow *caracol* staircase built into the north side of the facade—the work of one Fray Pedro de la Cruz, completed in 1562—gives access to both the balcony and the interior choir loft. The cornices of the gable curve steeply upwards to a spectacular espadaña with three bell openings—a modern addition. Pot pinnacles are set on the corners of the facade, as well as above the espadaña.

Many of the architectural features of the facade—cornices, scrolls, assorted openings and niches—are boldly accented in red and brown against the whitewashed stucco, lending a festive feeling to this essentially vernacular building.

If you have an interest in religious folk art, you should explore the church interior. Santos sacred to the unique Maya-Catholic cult of the Chamulas line both sides of a nave liberally strewn with pine needles during fiestas. In a heady haze of copal incense that fills the church, groups of Maya dressed in hand-woven apparel kneel in front of saints and crosses draped with ribbons and mirrors. Before the main altar are placed the images of John the Baptist (San Juan) and St. Michael (San Miguel), the patron saint of the musicians who often play in the church.

Note: Photography is strictly forbidden in the village and the church.

Numerous other mission churches are located in the rugged northeastern highlands of Chiapas, a region known in colonial times as Los Zendales. This name is a corruption of Tzeltal, one of two Maya languages spoken by the inhabitants, the other being Tzotzil.

Most of the churches have colonial origins and, although invariably altered, much of their fabric dates back hundreds of years. Three of the most accessible, **Huistán, Oxchuc** *and* **Ocosingo,** *are located in settlements along the scenic road from San Cristóbal to Palenque, the ancient Maya city in the Chiapas lowlands.*

San Miguel Huistán

SAN MIGUEL HUISTAN

Like Chamula, Huistán is a village of Tzotzil-speaking Maya. The settlement is perched on the side of a narrow ridge, overlooking the scenic valley below. The women of the village dress in white *huipiles* with floral embroidery and the men wear homespun wool ponchos against the highland chill. The mission of San Miguel was founded as a *visita* of the Dominican priory of Santo Domingo some time late in the 16th century, although it was later subject to the nearby monastery at Ocosingo.

As in all Maya villages, the church is the religious and social center of the community. It faces a large terraced plaza, undoubtedly the former mission atrium. At the far end of this plaza is mounted a traditional green tree cross, gaily bedecked with flowers and pine branches on feast days.

The modest church is built in the 16th century pueblo-de-indios style, with rubblestone walls and a pitched tile roof. Recently renovated, the powerful west front is similar to San Juan Chamula, with a conspicuous arched entry flanked by wall niches. Above the doorway, however, Huistán has a more clearly defined retablo facade, divided by prominent pilasters and cornices. Massive buttresses flare out on either side, visually integrated into the facade by inset niches and extension of the cornices.

Giant merlons, set on high pedestals and surmounted by enormous cannonball finials, flank the upper facade. Curving, scrolled cornices sweep up in front of the merlons, anchoring the upper pediment and supporting a freestanding espadaña. The crowning parapet is perforated by open brickwork—a decorative mudéjar touch in this otherwise rather austere folk-baroque facade.

The box-like nave contains a few altars, including a shrine to the Archangel Michael (San Miguel), the patron saint of the village, whose fiesta is celebrated in late September.

SANTO TOMAS OXCHUC

A little further along the road to Palenque, we pass Oxchuc, an impoverished Tzeltal village whose women still wear stunning red-and-white striped *huipiles*. The massive colonial church is a wounded giant. Its cracking walls and bowed wood-beamed roof are now undergoing much-needed repair. The most interesting features of the mission are its two surviving *posa* chapels, embedded in the surrounding atrium walls.

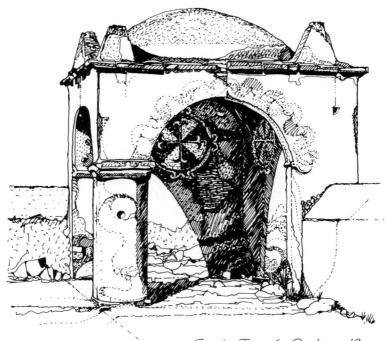

Santo Tomás Oxchuc, Posa chapel

Posa chapels were an essential element in the open-air missions of the Spiritual Conquest. Because of the large numbers of Indian converts in the early years, the first missions often consisted only of an enclosed atrium with a small sanctuary, or open chapel. Many of the sacraments, including baptism and the mass, were performed outdoors, and the friars would preach from the open chapel. Religious processions went around the atrium, pausing at the four corner chapels, or posas (from the Spanish: *posar* =to pause). The posas, with their own special saints, were sponsored and maintained by the native cofradías, becoming a vital part of community worship throughout the colonial era.

The posas at Oxchuc are the only ones still in place in Chiapas, apart from those at Tumbalá, a remote Maya village to the northeast, which were substantially redesigned in the last century. At Oxchuc, both posas are simple boxes, open on two sides and covered by low domes. Clearly visible on the inside wall of the southwest posa is the Dominican cross, still bearing traces of floral decoration. The position of the southeast posa, flush with the sanctuary arch inside the church, indicates that both chapels were part of the original mission, which probably consisted of little more than the present apse—used first as an open-air chapel and later as a self-contained church.

The barn-like nave, one of the largest in Chiapas, was added in the 1700s. It is faced by a broad retablo facade, expanded by curvetted side buttresses and crowned by a pediment of twin belfries flanking a central espadaña. On the festival of St. Thomas, held every year on December 21, Maya from the surrounding villages make a pilgrimage to the church to beseech the patron saint for rain.

San Jacinto Ocosingo

OCOSINGO

John Lloyd Stephens, the celebrated American explorer, passed through Ocosingo in 1840 and remarked on its "beautiful situation, surrounded by mountains, with a large church. In the center of the square was a magnificent *ceiba* tree."

Today, Ocosingo is a bustling ladino town located half way between the cool highlands and the *tierra caliente* of the eastern Chiapas lowlands. It is a jumping-off point for the spectacular Maya cities of Palenque and Toniná.

Although the giant ceiba has disappeared, the terraced plaza is pleasantly tree-shaded. The imposing church of San Jacinto still stands tall on the sunny eastern side. Despite radical rebuilding in the last century, the church continues to occupy the site of the last major Dominican monastery to be founded in Chiapas, the center of missionary activity in Los Zendales. Tzeltal Maya from nearby villages can often be seen in town, visiting the local market.

Remodeled in modern times, the striking west front has an abstract quality and reveals a definite folk-baroque influence. The tall center bay, which encloses the rounded doorway and choir window, is sharply recessed from the ground to the upper cornice, giving the facade a strong vertical emphasis. On either side, divided by ladder-like coffering, four tiers of paired niches with projecting corbels also reach to the full height of the facade.

The use of arcaded niches at Ocosingo echoes the facade of Coneta as well as the tower front at Comitán (see Chapter Two). The facade also recalls the magnificent west front of Coixtlahuaca, situated in northern Oaxaca, with its ranks of niches.

Although the large, well-lit interior has been modernized, with many of its surfaces faced with pebbles set in mortar, there is the usual complement of traditional folk altars at intervals along the nave.

Postscript. The scene of fierce fighting during the 1994 New Year rebellion, Ocosingo reportedly suffered considerable damage, including vandalism of the church.

CHAPTER TWO

COMITAN AND THE MISSION TOWNS OF SOUTHERN CHIAPAS

Temperate Comitán lies in the central plateau of Chiapas, a region known in colonial times as Los Llanos (The Plains). Despite the name, the terrain is varied, ranging from foggy highlands to the subtropical lowlands of the Grijalva River valley. Colonial art and architecture in this southern part of Chiapas are confined to religious buildings, primarily rural mission churches and a few surviving monasteries. While most of these monuments adhere to the styles familiar from elsewhere in Chiapas, they also reveal some distinctive local characteristics.

Itinerary

The Pan-American Highway winds southeast from San Cristóbal through pine-covered highlands, gradually descending towards Comitán. Half way between these two cities is a cluster of smaller towns and villages: **Teopisca**, **Amatenango** and **Aguacatenango**—all originally outlying Dominican visitas of Santo Domingo in San Cristóbal.

Each boasts its own unique church, built in the pueblo-de-indios style and containing rare colonial altarpieces. The main retablo at Teopisca is perhaps the outstanding example of baroque art extant in Chiapas. Just beyond Teopisca, near Amatenango, we go down a side road to the southwest, past Aguacatenango into the *tierra caliente* of the Grijalva River valley—a scenic journey through fields of corn and sugar cane that passes the rugged old mission at **Soyatitán** and terminates at the majestic abandoned monastery at **Copanaguastla**.

Comitán is a progressive town located on the Pan-American Highway. Its principal colonial monument is the church of Santo Domingo, which faces the huge main plaza. Several other churches of interest are to be found in the various city barrios, although most were rebuilt in post-colonial times. After Comitán, the highway winds south through dry hills and isolated former haciendas towards the Guatemalan border. Half way to the frontier stands the roadside village of **La Trinitaria**, built around its rustic hilltop church. We end this part of our journey at the solitary ruined monastery of **San José Coneta**—an architectural jewel isolated on a remote cattle ranch just a few kilometers from the border.

San Agustín Teopisca

TEOPISCA

Thomas Gage passed through Teopisca in 1626 on his way to Guatemala. He was favorably impressed, describing it as "a fair town of Indians [in which] nothing is so considerable as the church, which is great and strong and the music belonging unto it sweet and harmonious."

However, the only music to be heard on a recent visit was the sound of hammers and saws, for the entire church roof was being rebuilt. Although strengthened with steel supports, the new tiled roof, when complete, will resume its traditional form and appearance.

As Gage noted, the church at Teopisca, built about 1600, is larger and sturdier than most rural churches, being of stone and mortar throughout. With a large apse, it also boasts the largest nave of any church in Chiapas, with the exception of Oxchuc (see Chapter One). It is not clear why such an enormous space should have been needed as late as 1600, when the era of evangelization was over and the Indian population was already in decline. The historian Andrés Aubry has suggested that the nave may have functioned as a Christian necropolis, in order to restrict community burials to consecrated ground at a time when pagan funeral rites still persisted among the Maya.

Another explanation may be that, as the site of a prominent shrine to the ancient Mayan god-hero Votan, known as the "Red Lord," Teopisca continued to function as a place of pilgrimage for the highland Indians of Chiapas, after the Spanish Conquest and even into the 1600s. The bishops may have sponsored the construction of the church, furnishing it with imposing baroque retablos, in an attempt to channel native worship into orthodox Catholic channels. The continued popularity of the local festivals of San Sebastián and San Agustín seems to testify to the success of this policy.

The Facade

The monumental gabled facade, surmounted by an espadaña and domed belfries liberally studded with merlons, is typical of rural mission churches in Chiapas. But its most eye-catching feature is the giant blind arcade that runs across the lower facade, no doubt added to strengthen it after the devastating earthquake of 1817.

Set on high pedestals, the arcade frames the arched doorway and sculpture niches. Unfortunately, its architectural effectiveness is flawed, for by breaking in mid-arch at the corners, the arcade gives the impression that it continues around the corners and along the outside of the nave. It does not—although what a bold stroke that would have been!

The Retablos

The newly resplendent main altarpiece occupies the sanctuary of the renovated church. This great gilded retablo, originally from the church of San Agustín in San Cristóbal, is the earliest documented altarpiece in Chiapas, dated 1708 by an inscription. It was brought here in 1880, together with two smaller side retablos, to replace the altarpieces destroyed in the 1817 temblor.

We can be thankful that this superb altarpiece—the finest such colonial work to survive in Chiapas—has been preserved for posterity. It is a triumph of the Central American baroque style, comparable to the retablo of San José in the cathedral of San Cristóbal, which is also known to have come from San Agustín and was probably created in the same workshop.

The retablo fills the apse with its four broad tiers, which include the surmounting pediment and a broad predella, or base. Ranks of ornamental columns sumptuously frame the altarpiece, some intricately carved with twisted grapevines in the lavish Solomonic style and others overlain with ornate *diamante* designs. The opulence is enhanced by a dizzying variety of sculpted moldings, coffered cornices and relief panels of gilded foliage.

One of the more interesting components of the retablo is the elaborate predella, which is supported by Atlantean figures, dressed as archangels in boots and billowing robes. Angels and animal figures are also carved along the base, including what appears to be a jaguar on the extreme left.

The three center *calles*, or vertical bays of the altarpiece, enclose no less than twelve sculpture niches, many with scalloped canopies. All the niches harbor carved and painted statues, which diminish in size as the tiers ascend. Most of the figures are fine examples of colonial sculpture, with handsomely modeled features and brocaded draperies rendered in rich *estofado*.

Saints Peter and Paul take their places on the lower tier beside a modern image of St. Augustine. On the middle level, St. Francis and St. Dominic, the founders of the Mendicant missionary orders, flank the somber figure of the Virgin of the Rosary. As a reminder that this was

TEOPISCA The Main Retablo

1	St. Dominic	10	St. Dominic
2	St. Anne	11	Virgin of the Rosary
3	St. Rosalie	12	St. Francis of Assisi
4	St. Peter ? (P)	13	St. Hyacinth of Poland (P)
5	St. Francis de Borgia	14	Resurrection (P)
6	St. Ignatius Loyola	15	St. Paul
7	St. Francis Xavier	16	St. Augustine
8	Virgin of Mercy (P)	17	St. Peter
9	St. Augustine (P)	18	Nativity (P)

(P = painting)

Teopisca retablo, Statue of St. Francis Borgia

once the principal retablo of the Jesuit church in San Cristóbal, Ignatius Loyola, the Spanish founder of the Society of Jesus, occupies the center niche of the third tier between two other black-robed luminaries of the order, St. Francis Xavier and the aristocratic St. Francis Borgia.

A second figure of St. Dominic looks out from the top tier, flanked by St. Anne (left) and an antique processional statue of a Dominican nun (right). This statue of St. Dominic recently replaced an early colonial figure of St. Sebastian, a venerable image that may be older than the retablo itself and now rests, appropriately, in the nearby barrio chapel of San Sebastián. The altarpiece was originally commissioned by his namesake, Don Sebastián de Olivera Ponce de León, a prosperous merchant from San Cristóbal.

The outer bays of the retablo house six large painted panels, apparently assembled from more than one source. The two canvases on the lower tier are the most distinctive, showing an unmistakable Flemish Mannerist influence. On the left is a dramatic Resurrection, and on the right, an expressive Nativity scene. Portraits of various saints occupy the upper panels.

During the restoration of the church, a hitherto unknown altar was discovered behind the main retablo. This screen-like adobe structure, inset with niches and painted with floral motifs, was fitted into the rear of the apse and may once have served as the focal point of the 17th century sanctuary. Other furnishings, now stored in the sacristy, include some silver church plate and a relief of the Holy Trinity taken from one of the late 18th century retablos destroyed in the 1817 earthquake.

AMATENANGO DEL VALLE

This hilltop Tzeltal village overlooks the Pan-American Highway, some 5 kms past Teopisca. Best known for its traditional hand-made and wood-fired folk pottery displayed along the highway, Amatenango attracts many tourists, who are often besieged by pottery sellers—local Maya girls dressed in vivid red and yellow huipils and blue skirts.

A typical 17th century pueblo-de-indios church in plan, San Francisco Amatenango was largely rebuilt in the 18th century following a particularly severe earthquake. The fabric of the church is an amalgam of adobe, brick and rubblestone. Attractive tiles of various hues and textures overlay the beamed roof with its overhanging eaves.

The brilliant white churchfront with its red wooden doors faces the central plaza and is constructed of finely cut stone—rare indeed for a country church. The colonial retablo facade has been altered in modern times, losing some of its integrity in the process. The sharply silhouetted upper tier was added during the facelift, and much of the surface relief erased, giving the facade its present pristine look. However, vestiges of the old stucco ornament—mostly arabesques and scalloped decoration—have survived inside the sculpture niches.

A grid of ribbon pilasters and simple cornices crisscrosses the lower tiers of the facade, cleanly framing the rounded shapes of the niches, bell openings, stepped doorway and choir window. As a foil to this neat geometrical pattern, the stocky stone figure of St. Francis, Amatenango's patron saint, gazes down benignly from the central niche. The top tier rises well above the nave, drawing attention to the somewhat out-of-scale bell openings of the espadaña and domed belfries. The espadaña is appropriately capped with pottery urns.

Amatenango, Main retablo

A traditional wooden plank ceiling covers the dim nave, leading to an octagonal mudéjar vault over the sanctuary. Below this vault stands a provincial baroque altarpiece, painted in attractive Venetian red and greenish-blue hues. The retablo features a scalloped outline and gilded rocaille work in the Guatemalan style. Simple plateresque and spiral columns decorated with grapevines frame a group of naive canvases, including a crowded Nativity and several episodes from the life of St. Francis, whose festival is celebrated here in early October.

At Amatenango, a paved secondary road (Chis 101) heads southwest from the Pan-American Highway, winding down through purple hills and fields of brilliant green sugar cane towards the Grijalva River. This fertile region of the tierra caliente was a focus of early Spanish settlement and evangelization. Several buildings survive from this era, most notably the Dominican monastery at Copanaguastla. En route, we pass the villages of Aguacatenango and Soyatitán, and their rustic colonial churches.

AGUACATENANGO

Set at a distance from the highway beside a shallow seasonal lake, Aguacatenango has a more indigenous feeling than either Teopisca or Amatenango. Fishermen stand waist deep in the lake to cast their nets, while pigs and small children run through the narrow, rocky streets. Gleaming white huipils worn by the Maya women proudly showcase the village's unique style of embroidery.

The primitive church of Santiago looms protectively above the village from behind its narrow walled forecourt with a traditional green wooden cross. The rain-streaked west front seems like an archaic relic from the distant past. An uneven grid of crude pilasters and cornices divides the lower part while a craggy gable with domed belfries dominates the upper facade.

Numerous stucco reliefs, their details eroded by time and centuries of whitewashing, add to the rugged texture of the facade. A foliated cross is carved over the doorway and in the upper reaches, winged angels hover in a welter of shells, urns, scrolls, hearts and flowers. A battered figure—no doubt Santiago Matamoros, the patron of the church—gestures with upraised arms from a small niche just below the espadaña.

The church interior is surprisingly spacious, its nave roofed by a wooden ceiling painted in the locally favored colors of red and green. Red and green also predominate in the main altarpiece, another rustic baroque retablo related to the one we saw at Amatenango. Behind the retablo, researchers have discovered the remains of a painted wall altar with inset niches, similar to the one found at Teopisca.

Santiago Aguacatenango

SOYATITAN

Crowning the brow of a hill half way to Copanaguastla, the imposing stone churchfront of Asunción Soyatitán is a prominent local landmark. Today, however, much of the old mission is in ruins. The outer walls of the roofless nave, long exposed to the weather, have crumbled badly.

Although the sturdier rubblestone walls of the sanctuary block at the east end have resisted erosion, these too now show ominous cracks. The sanctuary window on the north side, with slender colonnettes fitted into its stepped jambs, is the only one to survive intact.

Founded in the 1560s, Soyatitán was the principal visita of the Dominican monastery at Copanaguastla. Much of the fabric dates back to the 16th century, although the church was extensively rebuilt following a catastrophic fire in 1641. Inside the old nave, the villagers have recently erected a small tin-roofed chapel which is used for catechism and occasional services.

The monumental west front is the best preserved part of the church, postdating the 1641 fire. Facing a secluded, grassy atrium, it measures almost nine feet in thickness. The three tiers of the broad retablo facade are effectively articulated by plain pilasters set between narrow, continuous cornices. Like the north window, the rounded central doorway and choir window are recessed behind multiple archways.

Rows of slender niches extend on either side of the main openings, embellished with supporting corbels and projecting scalloped arches. Above the facade rises a battered remnant of the monumental bell gable, originally stepped in the Flemish style, which even now retains enormous merlons on each corner.

A few token stucco urns and floral reliefs above the doorway constitute the only ornament in this strong but sober facade—an architectural composition of greater coherence and power than the rustic churchfronts we have viewed thus far in this region.

Asunción Soyatitán

COPANAGUASTLA

The great ruined monastery at Copanaguastla is among the most evoca-
tive 16th century monuments in Mexico. Abandoned less than a century
after its founding, the sturdily built church has survived almost 350 years
of neglect. Today it stands a silent but steadfast sentinel, watching over
the newly resettled village.

Soon after the Spanish Conquest, gold was discovered here in the hills
and streams above the Grijalva River. The subsequent rush made the
encomendero, Andrés de la Tovilla, a rich man, but devastated the
Tzeltal-speaking Maya settlement.

In 1545, four Dominicans arrived, led by Fray Domingo de Ara, an
energetic missionary and dedicated translator of devotional works into
Tzeltal. In spite of the environmental ravages wrought by gold mining,
the friars found the climate ideal—a veritable Jericho, as Fray Domingo
once observed. They gathered the surviving Maya together and built a
primitive thatched mission.

Following the official nomination of Copanaguastla as a priory in 1556,
erecting a permanent monastery became an urgent necessity. The project
went forward, supervised by the talented friar-architect Fray Francisco
de La Cruz, but in 1564, by a cruel stroke of fate, the virtually completed
church was struck by lightning. Hampered by famine and pestilence in
the community, reconstruction of the building continued only sporadi-
cally until 1568, when a stone vault at last replaced the charred wooden
roof—the final contribution of Fray Francisco who died in the same year.

By the end of the 16th century, Copanaguastla had become the principal
monastery for the region, and the friars were prospering from their sugar

Copanaguastla

cane plantations and cattle haciendas. Thomas Gage paid a memorable
visit here in 1625, when he "enjoyed much pastime and recreation among
the friars and Indians and was feasted after the manner of that country,
which knoweth more of an Epicurean diet than doth England."

But in 1629, another outbreak of the plague decimated the Indian population. Despite the great effort and expense that had been invested in its construction, the monastery was reluctantly abandoned. The friars moved to Socoltenango, near Soyatitán, taking with them the image of La Virgen del Rosario. In this higher, healthier location, the 16th century image (now known as La Candelaria), became the focus of popular pilgrimage during the later colonial years and into modern times.

The Church

The plan of the sturdy stone church is based on the Latin cross—unusual for monastic churches of this early period. Eroded buttresses brace its rubble walls, which are pierced at intervals by elongated, Romanesque windows. Part of a cracked belltower, which stood above the former convento, clings precariously to the surviving north transept.

Long since fallen, Fray Francisco's roof seems to have been constructed in distinct sections using a variety of contruction methods. The nave was spanned by a wooden artesonado roof resting on stone arches, one of which is still in place above carved corbels. An octagonal dome at one time stood on corner squinch arches above the crossing, flanked by two ribbed mudéjar vaults over the transepts. The sunken square apse at the east end may have been covered by a solid barrel vault, perhaps like that at the unfinished priory church of Cuilapan (Oaxaca). Fragments of the sanctuary arch, carved with shell niches, coffered panels and classical half columns, can still be seen at the crossing. Strangely, there is no evidence of the customary choir at the west end, possibly because the original wooden loft was not replaced after the 1564 thunderbolt.

The West Front

Angled corner buttresses, a structural feature first used in the early Dominican monastery of Oaxtepec (Morelos), neatly anchor the west front. Trees now sprout atop the facade where the gable formerly rose.

The squared facade is a plateresque composition, clearly related to Tecpatán (see Chapter Three) and the Dominican missions of Oaxaca. With the judicious use of cornices and pilasters, the various rounded arches and openings have been integrated into a harmonious classical design. On the lower tier, an elegant Italianate porch of fluted Tuscan pilasters frames the paneled doorway, which is inset with plain Renaissance medallions. Overhead, a frieze of winged cherubs links cameos of the bearded saints Peter and Paul. To either side of the porch are placed large arched niches with stepped frames like the nave windows.

A semicircular pediment rises above the porch, flanked by curious pinnacles carved with vases and grotesque miniature heads, and topped by fruit-and-flower finials. Narrow outer niches with corbeled brackets and delicate molded arches echo the larger openings below. Emblazoned in the corners of the upper facade are two relief escutcheons, encased in ornamental scrolls and carved with the *fleur-de-lis* cross of the Dominican order.

The once spacious convento has all but disappeared in recent years, save for a few crumbling archways and stone steps—a victim of the village reconstruction, for which it served as a quarry. Although the church remains roofless and overgrown, a crude stone altar and benches have recently been set up beneath the gaping crossing—a faint sign of religious revival after the long centuries of solitude.

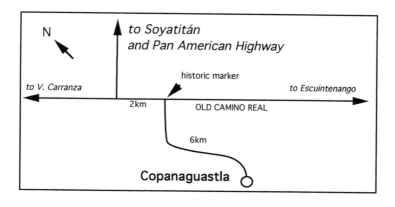

In colonial times, the Camino Real, or main road to Guatemala, ran through the Grijalva River valley instead of following the highland path of the present Pan American Highway. Several Dominican mission towns once stood along this route, notably **Escuintenango** *and its visitas of* **Coapa** *and* **Aquespala**.

Now well off the beaten track, these remaining mission churches languish in an advanced state of ruin. In Escuintenango, of the once substantial 16th century riverside church and convento only the south tower and fragments of the nave walls still stand. At Coapa, further to the southeast, the surviving adobe walls of the large church continue to erode into mud. And at Aquespala, near Coneta, mere vestiges remain of its once handsome classical facade.

Comitán

Comitán is a very clean town. Rows of young trees have been planted along the highway approaches and freshly painted wrought-iron benches line the leafy central plaza.

Originally founded in 1528 by Pedro de Portocarrero, one of Pedro de Alvarado's captains, the first settlement here was razed by his rival, Diego de Mazariegos. But in 1576, the town was rebuilt on higher ground, where it flourished as an important staging post on the Camino Real, the main Mexico to Guatemala route in the colonial era. A populous and prosperous frontier town into the 1840s, Comitán impressed the American explorer, John Lloyd Stephens, with its "superb church and well filled convent of Dominican friars." Today it is a flourishing market town and agricultural center.

SANTO DOMINGO DE COMITAN

On the east side of the plaza stands the impressive church dedicated to Santo Domingo (St. Dominic), the patron saint of Comitán. Designated a priory in 1596, this was the last of the Dominican monasteries to be established in Chiapas. During the colonial era, it presided over the numerous parishes of Los Llanos, a region that stretched southwards beyond the present border with Guatemala.

The church is very plain, in a provincial plateresque mode. The plaque inside the west porch, dated 1556, may commemorate the dedication of the early church, although construction continued by fits and starts well into the 17th century. The whitewashed west front facing the plaza consists of a spartan facade and the intriguing north tower. Surmounted by a broad curvetted gable, but unadorned by any sculptural reliefs, the severe facade is unlike any other in Chiapas. Its principal elements are a strongly projecting porch framing the arched entry, and a circular casement enclosing the octagonal choir window.

Its most striking feature is the tower, which rises by gradually diminishing stages, separated one from another by jutting cornices. A balustraded parapet, punctuated with cannonball merlons at each corner, surrounds the upper belfry. The geometric purity of the whitewashed tower was recently shattered by the discovery of several tiers of blind arcading beneath the surface stucco. Rudely fashioned in mudéjar or popular Romanesque style, they are undoubtedly part of the original

Santo Domingo de Comitán

fabric of the building. Carved reliefs, some representing the Dominican cross of Alcantara, have also been uncovered along the arcades. Although we see decorative arcading in the facade at Teopisca, Coneta and even on the cathedral in San Cristóbal, its sudden unveiling on the Comitán tower after centuries of oblivion adds an exciting new dimension to the early colonial architecture of Chiapas.

The old convento on the south side of the church has been replaced by a new brick structure housing a regional cultural center. A number of colonial artifacts from the church are on display, including a carved marble pulpit.

Other Comitán churches

Comitán is a city of churches. The Mayan name for the ridge upon which the city was built is Hill of the Nine Stars, a tradition reflected in the nine barrios of the city, each with its own church.

Many of these buildings are of special historic and architectural interest, but the only truly colonial church, apart from Santo Domingo, is the chapel of **San Sebastián Comitán**, which faces its own little plaza in an outlying artisans' barrio of the same name. During a recent facelift of the folk-baroque facade, several rustic colonial statues, mostly headless, were uncovered in previously walled-up niches. Four early paintings, believed to have come originally from Santo Domingo, hang inside the church.

Two other churches of colonial origin but rebuilt in later times are those of **El Calvario** and the neo-rococo temple of **San Caralampio.** St. Caralampio is an obscure saint of the early Christian church whose image was believed to have halted a plague in the 19th century. His cult still enjoys a strong regional following and his feast day is faithfully observed on February 11th.

By the early 1600s, Santo Domingo Comitán had numerous dependent visitas, some of which later became parishes in their own right. Few of these settlements, however, proved to be viable, especially those in the unhealthy tierra caliente, along the Grijalva River. Most were abandoned in colonial times and their monumental churches allowed to fall into ruin. Only in **La Trinitaria** is the church still intact and in daily use. Although abandoned, the roofless monastery at **San José Coneta** still retains its magnificent facade.

LA TRINITARIA

Fearful of being caught without a passport, John Lloyd Stephens hurried furtively through Zapaluta, as La Trinitaria was still known in 1839, noting its conspicuous church only in passing. Then as now, this was the first Mexican town encountered on the highway after crossing the frontier from Guatemala. In fact, it is the only settlement in the area that has been continuously populated since its founding in the late 16th century, probably because of its healthier elevation.

Today, La Trinitaria is a prosperous ladino town, located beside the Pan-American Highway 16 km southeast of Comitán. The church of the Holy Trinity overlooks a high, windswept central plaza—the former mission atrium—which commands a broad vista of the surrounding countryside including the Grijalva River basin and Cuchamatanes Mountains of Guatemala.

Although the former convento on the south side has been converted into a school, the church retains its colonial appearance and most of the original fabric. Much of the stonework at the sides and rear of the church is now exposed, revealing the time-honored technique of chinking—the use of stone chips inserted into the mortar between uneven courses of roughly cut stone, in order to strengthen the walls.

The nave and the unusual elevated polygonal apse are both covered by traditional tile roofs with overhanging eaves. Few furnishings of interest enliven the spare interior, save for a neoclassical altar of the Trinity, on which a benevolent God the Father, wearing his triple tiara, holds up the crucifix while the dove of the Holy Spirit hovers overhead.

Anchored on the corners by flat angled buttresses, the whitewashed retablo facade has a rustic vigor. Rude half columns and horizontal string courses mark out the tiers, enclosing simple rounded openings: the large doorway, a bull's eye window and several blank sculpture niches.

La Trinitaria

Rounded openings also predominate in the espadaña and belfries. The sole sculptural detail is a primitive relief of the Archangel Michael, mounted just below the espadaña. In one hand, the saint triumphantly brandishes his sword and in the other displays the banner of his victory over the forces of Satan.

CONETA

San José Coneta is an abandoned colonial town, situated in a hot, dry valley close to the Guatemalan border. The ruined church is a picturesque sight viewed from the entrance to the cattle ranch where it is located, its great gray stone hulk isolated in the middle of green pasture and tall stands of corn, silent except for the flutter of starlings and the rustle of crickets.

Dominican friars founded a mission town at Coneta late in the 16th century, resettling at least two Maya groups here. Initially a dependency of Copanaguastla, it was later attached to Santo Domingo de Comitán. Although parts of the mission seem to have been built at different times, the church and what little remains of the convento probably date from the mid- to late 1600s. Not long after its completion, however, the settlement steadily lost population and was permanently abandoned in 1804.

When John Lloyd Stephens stumbled across Coneta on his way to Palenque in 1839, the mission had been disused for more than thirty years, "a gigantic building, without a single habitation in sight. The facade was rich and perfect. It was . . . roofless, with trees growing out of the area above the walls. Nothing could exceed the quiet and desolation of the scene. We entered the open door of the church. The altar was thrown down, the roof lay in broken masses on the ground and the whole area was a forest of trees. At the foot of it . . . was a convent. There was no roof but the apartments were entire, as when a good padre stood to welcome a traveler. In front of the church, on each side, was a staircase leading up to a belfry in the center of the facade. We ascended to the top. The bells which had called to matin and vesper prayers were gone; the crosspiece was broken from the cross."

Although the church is roofless, its walls still stand and the extraordinary facade is remarkably well preserved after almost 200 years of neglect. Sturdily built of roughly dressed stone set in a matrix of lime mortar mixed with snail shells, the church ends in a polygonal apse braced by exterior angled buttresses. Stepped jambs and arches elegantly frame the nave windows and the interior is still partly faced with stucco. A tile-and-beam roof formerly stood above the nave, although a stone vault, now fallen, covered the sanctuary. Of the ruined convento, only the east range of the cloister survives, its crumbling arcades jutting out from the north side of the church.

San José Coneta

An exterior spiral stone staircase on the north side, now partly collapsed, led to the wooden choir loft—long since burned or dismantled—and ascended to the belfry. Recent attempts to find Stephens' initials, supposedly carved beside the belfry, have been thwarted by angry swarms of resident bees.

The Facade

Constructed of brick, stone and stucco, the broad west front was conceived, built and ornamented as a distinct architectural unit separate from the rest of the church. The striking retablo facade has been transformed by its unique style of ornament into an original example of folk-plateresque design.

There are no less than five tiers, each with its own architectural treatment and applied ornament. A large central doorway dominates the bottom tier. The door frame is stepped back behind a sequence of archways, which preserve traces of painted decoration. Recognizable subjects include angels, crosses and foliage with maize and other indigenous plants, all executed in blue and reddish-brown. Alternating button and lozenge reliefs decorate the outer archway—a motif that repeats along the arcades of cushioned pilasters on either side of the doorway. The arcading also serves to frame a set of four elongated niches with scalloped arches. Little quatrefoil reliefs in boxed frames peek out between the arches.

Less conventional niches and pilasters alternate across the facade on the second level. Here, the pilasters are more elaborate, with curved and triangular sections punctuated by assorted holes, sunburst reliefs, drum moldings and consoles. Spool-and-spiral jambs, possibly derived from the relief crosses on the tower of Santo Domingo in Comitán, frame the six intervening niches, which are capped with yoke-like headers and surmounted by what appear to be projecting urns or barrel corbels. Another tiny niche, flanked by more button reliefs, is inset above the bull's eye window in the center facade.

The shallower third level repeats, with variations, the pattern of the second tier. Stubby cushioned pilasters, headed by block capitals and faced with miniature coffers and spools, alternate with small square niches. These mudéjar niches are elaborately framed by pairs of candelabra half columns and lobed headers with serrated horseshoe arches.

The upper gable and flanking belfries have lost most of their stucco facing. Again, cushioned pilasters divide the lower part of the gable,

enclosing shell niches that still contain the mutilated statues of uniden-
tified saints. Ringed half columns frame the belfries and the espadaña,
which has unfortunately lost its handsome scrolls and finials.

The sources of the eclectic ornamentation of the Coneta facade are
unclear. Although some of the motifs derive from mudéjar, plateresque
and even baroque decoration, there is more than a hint of indigenous or
even pre-hispanic influence in their forms and application; a small Maya
archaeological site has been discovered nearby.

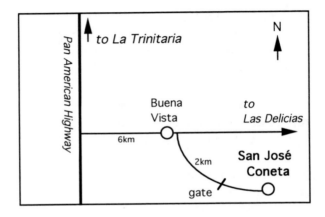

*We end our exploration of southern Chiapas at San José Coneta, whose long-
abandoned church exemplifies the neglect of much of the region's historic
architecture. The nearby colonial church of **Aquespala**, another abandoned
mission town, on the banks of the San Gregorio river, has now almost
disappeared except for a section of its once grand facade—another sad
example of indifference to the past.*

*Although several colonial monuments of Chiapas have been stabilized
or even restored under the supervision of federal, state or community conserva-
tion agencies, many of its rural buildings continue to deteriorate at an
accelerating pace as the countryside becomes more densely settled.*

CHAPTER THREE

CHIAPA DE CORZO AND THE MISSIONS OF NORTHERN CHIAPAS

Northern Chiapas is one of the most scenic regions in the state. Although its waters have now been tamed by a succession of dams, the mighty Grijalva River remains the dominant feature of the area. Gathering strength as it winds through its upper valley, the river breaks dramatically through the last of the highland ridges, surging north through the narrow Sumidero Canyon.

Settled in ancient times by the Zoques, a non-Maya people, this region was the theater of repeated incursions by northern invaders: first the belligerent Chiapanecs, then the Aztecs and finally, the Spaniards. In 1524 Bernal Díaz del Castillo passed through the area, describing the Chiapanec capital of Chiapan as "truly a city, with well laid out streets and houses and over 4000 inhabitants." The first colonial town to be established in Chiapas after the Spanish Conquest was located close to Chiapan, and was known as Chiapa de Indios.

Architecturally, the colonial buildings of northern Chiapas fall into the plateresque tradition of the early period, infused with a powerful mudéjar influence from southern Spain. The urban buildings of Chiapa de Indios were complemented by the Dominican missions of the Zoque hinterland, notably those at Copainalá and Tecpatán.

Church towers, rare elsewhere in Chiapas, are much in evidence in this region, often taking unusual and original forms. Towers were costly luxuries and in early colonial times explicitly forbidden in monastic buildings. Conversely, we see few of the soaring retablo facades that predominated in the highlands. The retablo facade, usually surmounted by an espadaña, belfries, or both, generally made the bell tower unnecessary.

Chiapa de Corzo

In March 1528, Diego de Mazariegos founded the first Spanish settlement here. Named Villa Real de Chiapa, it briefly served as the first capital of the new colony. Unhappy with the enervating climate and the abundant mosquitos, the Spaniards soon decided to move their capital up into the cooler highlands. Nevertheless, a few Spanish settlers elected to remain behind and within a few years, the small community of encomenderos and traders was prospering from agriculture and the lucrative cacao bean trade. Still a predominantly Indian town, it became known as Chiapa de Indios. In 1545, the colonists invited the Dominicans here to evangelize the indigenous Chiapanecs, Zoques, and native troops from central Mexico who had settled here after the Spanish Conquest.

This hospitable gesture, in contrast to the hostility of the Spanish residents of Ciudad Real, encouraged the friars, led by Bartolomé de Las Casas himself, to set about the tasks of converting the Indians and building a mission here. By 1550, Chiapa was rapidly becoming a major Dominican mission town. The 1570s saw the mission of Santo Domingo raised to the status of a priory and the subsequent construction of a substantial monastery. The church of San Sebastián was also rising on a hill overlooking the burgeoning riverside settlement and an aqueduct was bringing fresh spring water to the new fountain in the plaza.

Even today, in contrast to Tuxtla Gutiérrez, the modern state capital across the river, Chiapa de Corzo—the town was renamed yet again in the 1800s—has kept much of its colonial character. A low-rise settlement stretched out along the river bank and spreading comfortably into the surrounding hills, its colonial style houses fringe the enormous main plaza, which is still dominated by the fountain, the town's most prominent structure.

The Fountain at Chiapa de Corzo

THE FOUNTAIN

Towering over the main plaza at Chiapa de Corzo, this magnificent brick structure is one of the most spectacular 16th century monuments to survive in all of Mexico. Completed in 1562, the fountain has been attributed to the Dominican friar, Fray Rodrigo de Leon, who may also have planned the aqueduct that fed it. Its architecture draws on mudéjar (Hispano-Moorish) motifs and building methods, to create a functional and striking design that is unique in the Americas.

The fountain is all the more remarkable for its excellent state of preservation, the result of painstaking restoration. Indeed, its appearance seems to have changed little since the Franciscan Alonso Ponce passed through here in 1586, praising it as "beautiful, built of brick and vaulted with fifteen arches and a spiral staircase, and a great basin into which water cascades from a multitude of pipes . . ."

The structure is formed entirely of orange bricks, some custom-shaped for decorative purposes. Its design is based on the octagon, a mudéjar motif common in southern Spain. The central pavilion, supported on an octagonal arcade, encloses an eight-sided basin and surrounding raised walkway.

The vault is a spectacular hemispherical dome, topped by an ornamental brick lantern. Inside the dome, Gothic-style ribs spring from the corner piers of the arcade, terminating in an octagonal boss at the apex. From there, brick courses radiate downwards in ever widening circles, creating a visually stunning and structurally powerful pattern.

Flying buttresses, another Gothic feature, brace the eight corners to form an outer arcade. The octagonal motif extends to the polygonal columns attached to the piers and the upper sections of the buttresses. The turreted stair tower on the north side may have been the model for the *caracol* stairways found in many of the mission churches of the region, notably those at Tecpatán and Copainalá.

In the Islamic tradition, there is no representation of human or animal figures; geometric patterns of decoration prevail. Alternating bricks project around the archways to produce a horseshoe effect, another mark of the fountain's Moorish pedigree.

Rusticated diamond panels—on the jambs of the arcade, across the upper faces of the tower, and along the crowning parapets and finials—contribute to the rich texture and cast constantly changing shadows in the play of the tropical sunlight. More ornamental brickwork atop the buttresses, corner finials and the turret of the stairway add the crowning touches to this extraordinary building.

SANTO DOMINGO

At its zenith early in the 17th century, the Dominican chronicler Antonio de Remesal described the priory of Santo Domingo in glowing terms as "one of the best of our Order in New Spain. The church is large and strong with three naves, all of brick. The *capilla mayor* [sanctuary] is most sightly, of good proportion and furnished with retablos. The cloister is well built, with spacious cells overlooking the river. Because of the generosity of the priors, the sacristy is well endowed with rich ornaments of greater value than anywhere else."

As soon as he arrived in 1545, Bartolomé de Las Casas founded the first Dominican monastery in Chiapas. This rambling adobe and thatch structure rose quickly beside the river under the direction of the multi-talented Fray Tomás de la Torre. By the time the mission became a priory in 1576, the original buildings were already being replaced by a perma-nent masonry church and convento, supervised by an energetic new prior, Pedro de Barrientos.

Today, the great basilican church, known locally as the Cathedral, is all that survives of the 16th century priory. Even so, the imposing brick building has been significantly altered over the centuries, especially in recent decades, sacrificing some of its original appearance in the process. The riverside convento was unfortunately demolished in the 1800s.

The Basilica

Similar in many respects to the arcaded basilica at Cuilapan in Oaxaca— a contemporary Dominican building—the church of Santo Domingo features a nave and side aisles built to almost the same height and divided by plain, two-story arcades set on octagonal piers. High above the whitewashed arcades, dark wood-beamed roofs cover the nave and aisles. Recently reconstructed to simulate the 16th century originals, the new ceilings have done much to restore the attractive colonial ambience of the interior.

The rectangular apse at the east end and its two small flanking chapels are thought to belong to the 16th century fabric, perhaps as part of an open chapel that predated the church itself. All three spaces are vaulted by low domes with decorative Gothic ribs—more modest versions of the dome over the fountain and possibly built by the same team of masons. The

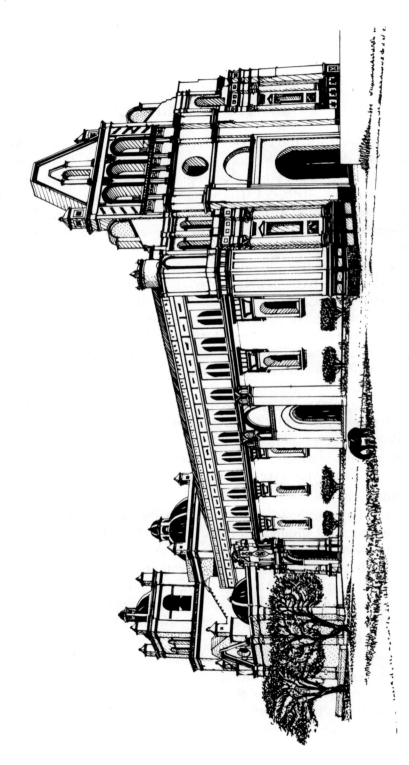

Santo Domingo de Chiapa de Corzo

north and south transepts are later, but follow the pattern set by the apsidal chapels. The dome over the crossing, however, seems to date from the 18th century, as do the classical friezes along the nave and the Dominican escutcheon above the sanctuary arch. The date 1554 beside the insignia may refer to the dedication of the primitive mission, since little of the present basilica could have been built by such an early date.

Virtually nothing survives of the gilded retablos that formerly graced the interior, all sadly replaced by characterless neoclassical altars in the 19th century. A single fragment from the 16th century main altarpiece, however, has been preserved under glass in the nearby chapel of **El Calvario**, a picturesque folk-Gothic building located in a hillside barrio of the same name. Probably the centerpiece of the lost retablo, this stunning polychrome relief of the Descent from the Cross is tightly composed and carved in the popular medieval style of northern Europe—crowded with gesturing figures in robes with sharply delineated folds.

The exterior is imposing from almost any viewpoint. From the gabled west front, the nave and aisles sweep eastwards. Boldly mullioned windows and ornamental brick cornices—all modern additions—run the length of the upper nave wall, while baroque curlicues, heavily outlined in brown, arch over the aisle windows.

At the east end is a cluster of tower and chapel blocks—a bold geometry of ribbed domes, pyramidal merlons, angular pediments and cornices in brilliant white stucco, pierced by dark rounded archways and niches. The massive tower, not unlike that of El Carmen in San Cristóbal, was added in the late 1600s. Inside the tower hangs a great bell inscribed with the date 1576. Its particularly sonorous tone is attributed to the gold that according to local legend was added to the bell metal.

The two entries on the north side present a study in contrasts. The plain westerly portal is a simplified version of the elaborate facade portada— an arched doorway with a semicircular lunette above, framed by broad pilasters.

The second entry, beside the north transept, combines baroque sophistication with popular whimsy; paired Ionic columns flank the doorway, changing above the molded entablature into fluted pilasters supporting a curvetted pediment. The outline of a stylized monstrance—or is it the Dominican cross of Alcántara?—appears in the pediment, flanked by fluted pinnacles crowned with coronets.

The Facade

Newly accented in brown paint against brilliant white stucco, the striking west front looks as if it has been fabricated from children's building blocks. Actually, the facade is an assemblage of diverse stylistic elements, transformed over time but still unified by its fundamentally 17th century form.

The focus of the composition is the elongated central porch. The oldest part of the facade, it is a starkly abstract relative of the grand Oaxacan portadas at Yanhuitlan and Cuilapan. Giant pilasters linked by molded cornices securely frame the doorway, whose rounded arch is echoed in the blank lunette and again in the circular window above. A blind colonnade with outsize classical dentils serves as a base for the broad espadaña overhead. Three Isabelline bell openings, topped by a truncated triangular pediment of baroque inspiration but recent construction, are flanked by ornamental coffered merlons.

The Palladian-style wings of the facade are the result of an 18th century remodeling—in all likelihood replacing the original aisle doorways of the basilica. A coffered pier-buttress on the north corner encloses a spiral stairway. A procession of turrets, belfries, raised niches and half pediments ascend on either side of the central espadaña, endowing this already wildly eclectic churchfront with an even more fanciful silhouette.

SAN SEBASTIAN

St. Sebastian (San Sebastián) is one of the most popular saints in Chiapas. Almost every town has a church or chapel dedicated to him. Why St. Sebastian is so prominent here is something of a puzzle. Perhaps his appeal springs from his medieval reputation as a protector against the plague and other epidemics—notorious scourges during colonial times. The indigenous people also associate this Christian martyr with the widespread pre-hispanic practice of *Tlacacaliliztli*, or arrow sacrifice.

Since St. Sebastian was an early patron of the Indian community in Chiapa de Corzo, his feast day is the most important and colorful festival in the religious calendar. Starting on January 6th and climaxing on January 23rd, a variety of masked figures—including *chuntaes* (dancers with fruit-laden headresses) and *parachicos* (bewigged flagbearers)—cavort through the city streets amid great revelry.

San Sebastián

Besides Santo Domingo, the outlying ruined basilica of San Sebastián is the only other surviving colonial church in Chiapa de Corzo. Built during the 1600s on a rocky promontory overlooking the town, the valley and the river, it was intended as the *parroquía*, or parish church, for the large indigenous population of the town. The Indians long complained about its inconvenient location so that by the late 1700s, following a successful lawsuit, Santo Domingo once again became the parroquía for the community.

With this reversal, however, San Sebastián fell into disuse and neglect, a condition from which it has never really recovered. Because of its commanding site, the church was used as a fortified lookout in the 19th century. In recent years, an outdoor chapel dedicated to the Virgin of Guadalupe has been erected beside the battlemented sanctuary—which also may have begun life as an open-air chapel from which the early friars preached to the assembled Indians.

Statue of St. Sebastian

In plan, San Sebastián borrows the basilican form of Santo Domingo, although it has no crossing or transepts and only reaches a single story in height. The side walls have collapsed, although a few of the octagonal brick piers that supported the interior arcades still poke through the weeds sprouting along the rubble-strewn nave. The wooden roof that once covered the nave has long since collapsed, together with the mudéjar dome that once vaulted the massive sanctuary block, whose corners still carry the stumps of rugged merlons.

The broad stone and brick facade has been partially restored, although it still lacks its stucco veneer and surmounting gable. Transitional in style between the Plateresque missions of lowland Chiapas and the popular retablo facades of the highlands, the west front of San Sebastián recalls the facade of the distant basilica at Cuilapan and may echo the original facade of neighboring Santo Domingo.

Colossal half columns, set on high pedestals, divide the facade into three wide bays. Breaking through the cornice separating the two main tiers, the columns also frame the arched central doorway and choir window. Paired blank niches occupy the lateral bays on both tiers. Massive projecting piers, perhaps originally intended as towers, anchor the facade at either end. Unfortunately, only a few fragments of the great triangular gable now protrude above the facade; the soaring central espadaña has entirely eroded, together with the belfries that at one time capped the towers.

With the reinstatement of Santo Domingo as the parish church of Chiapa de Indios in the 18th century, all the furnishings of San Sebastián were moved down the hill along with the Indian congregation. One of the few surviving relics is the venerable statue of San Sebastián, which is now kept in Santo Domingo and displayed in all its richly embroidered finery each year during the January celebrations.

Missions of the Zoque Country

This rugged region of northern Chiapas stretches along the Grijalva River basin beyond the Sumidero Canyon, through the low westerly ridges of the central highlands and into the plain beyond.

The Zoque-speaking Indians of the area offered little resistance to pacification and even acted as allies of the Spaniards during their conquest of the Chiapanecs. But it was not until 1549 that Dominican friars ventured forth to evangelize the region. Missionaries led by Fray Alonso de Villalba began to congregate the Indians into mission towns.

The largest of these settlements was at Tecpatán, which for almost 200 years was the center of Dominican activity in the Zoque Country. At its height, the grand priory of Tecpatán commanded a host of dependent visita missions: at Copainalá, Quechula, Tapalapa and other settlements. But apart from Tecpatán, the church at Copainalá is the only other early Dominican mission building to survive in the region.

Today, both Tecpatán and Copainalá are easily reached from Tuxtla Gutiérrez, along a scenic new paved road that crosses the Grijalva River at the Chicoasén Dam.

COPAINALA

Founded as a mission town in the 1550s, Copainalá sits picturesquely along a ridge, higher and dryer than Tecpatán down the road. The highway bypasses Copainalá on the far side of a ravine, affording a panoramic view of the terraced streets and the spectacular ruined colonial church, known to locals as La Ruina.

The settlement prospered during the late 1500s, evidently justifying the construction of a large church and convento. Of the original monastery only the church remains, mutilated and abandoned. The convento on the north side was demolished and its site is now occupied by a schoolyard and the small 19th century parish church of San Miguel.

The period of church construction was a lengthy one, from circa 1570 to the mid-1600s, which may explain the variety of building materials and stylistic anomalies. Stucco originally covered most of the interior

San Miguel Copainalá

and exterior surfaces, but has fallen away to reveal the underlying fabric. Roughly quarried stone predominates in the lower walls of the church, changing to brick in the upper elevations.

Raised on a terraced stone plaza—its former atrium—the church faces west across a steeply sloping *barranca*. Presently, the nave ends at the crossing. The former apse, which cut into the hillside at the east end, has collapsed or been demolished, leaving behind a gaping hole currently filled with rubble. The transepts still stand, along with two small adjoining chapels. Pitched beam-and-tile roofs at one time covered the now roofless church except for the apse, which was vaulted in stone.

As noted earlier, churches in northern Chiapas are conspicuous for their towers, an attribute generally lacking in other parts of the state. The tower at Copainalá, a massive square structure adjoining the south side of the facade, is the most unusual feature of the church. Although it may lack the more exotic aspects of the tower at Tecpatán, it has its own distinctive characteristics. These include a huge blind archway of unknown purpose on the south face and a circular brick stairway, tucked into the corner behind the tower. The stairway employs decorative mudéjar brickwork and a castellated turret strikingly similiar to the stair tower of the fountain at Chiapa de Corzo.

As elsewhere in the region, monumental pilasters buttress the west front of the church. Here mounted on high pedestals, they frame the entry portico, rising to meet the broad triangular gable that stands atop the facade. The pilasters terminate in outsize obelisks, also set on pedestals. A third obelisk surmounts the central gable, which is pierced by a small rose window that still preserves fragments of tracery.

The 17th century Italianate portico takes the form of a triumphal arch, elegantly framing the west doorway with paired pilasters and urn-like pinnacles that echo the obelisks atop the facade. The attic above the doorway retains traces of a Latin inscription referring to St. Michael, the patron saint of Copainalá.

TECPATAN

In 1940, Heinrich Berlin "rediscovered" the magnificent priory of Santo Domingo Tecpatán. After flying into Copainalá—an adventure in itself—the intrepid archaeologist and art historian undertook the seven hour mule trip onwards to Tecpatán, a jolting journey across rugged terrain of steep ridges and heavily wooded barrancas.

These days Tecpatán is much easier to discover, located only twenty minutes by car along a well-engineered blacktop highway from Copainalá. The mossy hulk of the 16th century priory still broods above its overgrown atrium in the center of this tropical hillside town—a magnificent but timeworn monument to faded Dominican hopes and missionary efforts among the Zoques.

In January 1564, the primitive thatched adobe structure built by the first friars at Tecpatán was chosen to be the principal mission for the Zoque area. Fray Antonio de Pamplona, a brilliant linguist and man of culture, was dispatched to start work on a permanent church and convento assisted by Rodrigo de León, who by then had finished work on the fountain at Chiapa de Corzo. Construction, however, was still going on in 1572 and, even when Tecpatán was elevated to a priory in 1595, the building remained unfinished.

Stylistically, the monastery belongs to the late 16th century. An imposing and original building, it draws on the diverse architectural traditions current at that formative period—late medieval, mudéjar, plateresque and Renaissance.

The Church

The canyon-like nave, now open to the sky, was originally spanned by a pitched artesonado roof supported on masonry arches, some of which still rest precariously in place. A massive double archway at the west end, that once supported a choir loft, springs from the ground and curves across the nave. At the east end, a short flight of steps leads up to the narrow apse, which is framed by a classical archway. This is surmounted by a Moorish *alfiz* and vaulted by a scalloped half dome—the only remaining roof section in the church. In contrast, the cavernous sacristy, beside the apse, is roofed by a lofty Gothic vault in a ribbed cloverleaf pattern.

Several openings and niches, variously framed, pierce the nave on both sides. An inconspicuous plateresque doorway gives access to the

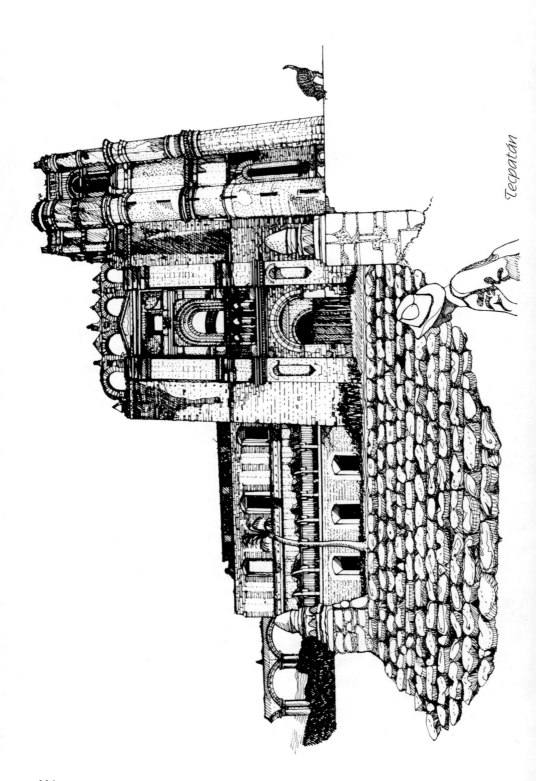

Tecpatán

tower in the southwest corner. But the most prominent of these openings is the grand south porch of the church. Broad pilasters topped with plateresque finials frame the exterior as part of a "door-within-a-door" design, related to the north entry at Yanhuitlan—the great Dominican priory in Oaxaca.

A second set of pilasters flanks the archway, enclosing a Renaissance-inspired inner doorway, and the Dominican insignia are emblazoned on a crumbling stucco panel above.

The West Front

Once again, giant Tuscan pilasters frame the entire center facade. These are quite plain apart from shallow shell niches embedded at eye level, which are reminiscent of the churchfront at Teposcolula, another major Dominican monastery in the Mixteca Alta region of Oaxaca.

The grand brick and stone churchfront has lost much of its stucco veneer. The simple arched doorway retains only vestiges of its fluted surround and worn Corinthian pilasters flank the handsome choir window overhead. A row of blank sculpture niches separates the doorway and choir window. These are sandwiched between dentilled cornices that continue across the flanking pilasters—a characteristic signature of Dominican architecture. A shallow triangular pediment caps the center facade. The crumbling espadaña is a later addition—a picturesque silhouette of looping arches capped with eroded baroque pediments and finials.

The Tower

As at Copainalá, the extraordinary tower is the most striking feature of this church. Even more fantastical in design, with turret-like buttresses at the corners, the tower conjures up the image of a medieval castle.

A rounded buttress anchors the southeast corner while an imposing octagonal buttress braces the southwest corner of the tower. The cylindrical turret projecting from west face encloses a narrow caracol stairway illuminated by slit openings. Beside the stairway, a narrow Romanesque window illuminates the former baptistry located within the tower.

The vaulted belfry retains traces of murals that include biblical subjects, religious symbols and floral ornament—decoration that must originally have adorned almost every surface in the church and monastery.

Tecpatán, The upper cloister

The Convento

Tecpatán is the only monastery in Chiapas to retain even part of its original cloister, a grandiose two-story structure distinguished by elegant arcades of burnt-orange brick. Tragically, much of the west side of the convento, including a former posa chapel, collapsed in a recent earthquake and only the east and south ranges have been reconstructed.

The few intact upper rooms are used as parish offices, accessible via a monumental stairway with another cloverleaf vault and walls decorated with faded Dominican emblems entwined in foliage. The cloister walks are covered by lofty brick groin vaults and faced by arcades with paneled piers. Along the upper arcade, plain and spiral colonnettes are attached to the inner faces of the piers—a method reminiscent of the early Dominican cloister at Oaxtepec (Morelos).

Threatened by accelerating deterioration and possible collapse, the fabric of both church and convento was stabilized and partially repaired in the early 1970s, helping to preserve this grand monument for, we may hope, fuller restoration in the future.

Numerous other colonial missions and churches at one time dotted the Zoque country. Some still stand, although altered beyond recognition by later reconstruction, at Chapultenango, Coapilla, Sayula, Tapalapa, Tapilula and Usumacinta.

Others lie in ruins or have disappeared altogether, victims of time and the elements, as well as man-made disasters. The elegant Dominican church at Quechula, for example, only recently disappeared beneath the dammed-up waters of the Grijalva River, while the rustic church at Ostuacán to the east was a casualty of the 1982 eruption of the Chichonál volcano.

ILLUSTRATIONS

La Quinta del Aserradero   Page 2
Bartolomé de Las Casas   6
The fountain stairway, Chiapa de Corzo   9
Map of Chiapas   10
La Sirena, Mermaid relief   23
Map of San Cristóbal de Las Casas   24
San Cristóbal, the Cathedral   28
The Cathedral, Statue of San José   31
San Cristóbal, San Nicolás   33
San Cristóbal, La Casa de la Sirena   35
Santo Domingo de San Cristóbal   38
Statue of Santiago (Los Altos Museum)   42
San Cristóbal, La Caridad   44
San Cristóbal, Tower of El Carmen   46
San Cristóbal, San Francisco   49
San Cristóbal, San Agustín   51
The Cuxtitali Bridge   54
Cuxtitali   56
San Cristóbal, San Diego   58
San Felipe Ecatepec   60
La Quinta Chapel   62
San Juan Chamula, from San Sebastián   66
San Miguel Huistán   68
Santo Tomás Oxchuc, Posa chapel   70
San Jacinto Ocosingo   71
San Agustín Teopisca   74
Teopisca, Main retablo (plan)   77
Teopisca retablo, Statue of St. Francis Borgia   78
Amatenango, Statue of St. Francis   80
Amatenango, Main retablo   81
Santiago Aguacatenango   83
Asunción Soyatitán   85
Copanaguastla   87
Santo Domingo de Comitán   91
La Trinitaria   94
San José Coneta   96
The Fountain at Chiapa de Corzo   101
Santo Domingo de Chiapa de Corzo   104
San Sebastián de Chiapa de Corzo   107
Santo Domingo, Statue of St. Sebastian   108
San Miguel Copainalá   111
Santo Domingo Tecpatán   114
Tecpatán, the upper cloister   116

SELECT BIBLIOGRAPHY

Artigas, Juan B. *La arquitectura de San Cristóbal de Las Casas.* Mexico City: Universidad Nacional Autónoma de México (UNAM), 1991.

Aubry, Andrés. *San Cristóbal de Las Casas, historia urbana demográfica y monumental.* San Cristóbal de Las Casas: Instituto de Asesoría Antropológica para la Región Maya, A.C. (INAREMAC), 1991.

———. *El templo de Teopisca.* San Cristóbal de Las Casas: INAREMAC 1993.

Berlin, Heinrich. "El convento de Tecpatán." *Anales del Instituto de Investigaciones Estéticas* #3 (UNAM), 1942.

Bernal Díaz del Castillo. *Historia de la conquista de Nueva España.* Mexico City: Editorial Porrua, 1976.

Blom, Frans. "El retablo de Teopisca en Chiapas." *Anales del Instituto de Investigaciones Estéticas* #25 (UNAM), 1955.

Bricker, Victoria R. *The Indian Christ, the Indian King.* Austin: University of Texas Press, 1981.

Chamberlain, Robert S. *The Governorship of the Adelantado Francisco de Montejo in Chiapas, 1539-1544.* Washington, DC: Carnegie Institute Publications #46, 1958.

Flores Ruiz, Eduardo. *La Catedral de San Cristóbal de Las Casas 1528-1978.* Tuxtla Gutiérrez: Universidad Nacional Autonoma de Chiapas (UNACH), 1978.

Gage, Thomas. *A New Survey of the West Indies, 1648.* London: Routledge and Sons, 1946.

Gerhard, Peter. *The Southeast Frontier of New Spain.* Princeton: Princeton University Press, 1979.

Gosner, Kevin. *Soldiers of the Virgin: The Moral Economy of a Colonial Maya Rebellion.* Albuquerque: University of New Mexico Press, 1992.

Humberto Ruz, Mario. *Copanaguastla en un espejo.* San Cristóbal de Las Casas: UNACH , 1985.

MacLeod, Murdo J. and Robert Wasserstrom, eds. *Spaniards and Indians in Southwestern Mesoamerica.* Lincoln: University of NebraskaPress, 1983.

Markman, Sidney David. *Architecture and Urbanization in Colonial Chiapas, Mexico.* Philadelphia: American Philosophical Society, 1984.

Perry, Richard D. *Mexico's Fortress Monasteries.* Santa Barbara: Espadaña Press, 1992.

Perry, Richard D. and Rosalind W. Perry, *Maya Missions.* Santa Barbara: Espadaña Press, 1988

Pulida Solís, Maria Trinidad. *Historia de la arquitectura en Chiapas.* Mexico City: Instituto Nacional de Antropología e Historia (INAH), Serie: Historia, 1990.

Remesal, Fray Antonio de. *Historia general de las Indias ... Chiapa y Guatemala.* (1642) Madrid: Ediciones Atlas (2 vols), 1966.

Stephens, John Lloyd. *Incidents of Travel in Central America, Chiapas and Yucatan.* (2 vols). New York: Harper & Brothers, 1841.

Vos, Jan de. *San Cristóbal: ciudad colonial.* Mexico City : INAH, 1986.

———. *Los enredos de Remesal.* Mexico City: Consejo Nacional para la Cultura y las Artes, 1992.

Wasserstrom, Robert. *Class and Society in Central Chiapas.* Berkeley: University of California Press, 1983.

GLOSSARY

adelantado. Military commander or governor of a newly conquered colonial province.

alfiz. Squared frame above an opening, a mudéjar architectural device.

arabesque. Complex decorative motif, originally of Islamic origin.

artesonado. Wooden roof or ceiling of Islamic origin; traditionally with carved beams (*zapatas*) and occasionally embellished with coffering and inlaid decoration or painting.

atrium. An enclosed churchyard or forecourt.

baluster. Decorative treatment of a column derived from turned wood designs.

barranca. Narrow ravine or canyon.

barrio. Quarter or district of a Mexican colonial town.

cacao. Cocoa beans from which chocolate is manufactured; used as currency by the ancient and colonial Maya.

calle. 1. Street. 2. Vertical band in a colonial altarpiece.

capilla mayor. The sanctuary of the church, where the altar is located.

caracol. Enclosed spiral staircase, from the Spanish word for snail.

ceiba. The giant silkcotton tree, native to the Maya region; the "Tree of the World".

chiaroscuro. The play of light and shade.

Churrigueresque. Descriptive term for the ornate Mexican late baroque style in architecture, loosely associated with the Spanish architects, the Churriguera brothers.

cofradía. Religious fraternity or brotherhood.

coleto. Colloquial term for a resident of San Cristóbal de Las Casas.

console. Carved, ornamental architectural bracket; *see also* corbel.

copal. An aromatic incense made from hardened tropical tree resins.

corbel. A supporting stone or wooden bracket, or console.

Corinthian. The most ornate of the classical orders of columns, usually headed by a scrolled capital with acanthus leaves.

dentil. Tooth-like ornament, derived from classical architecture.

diamante. Diamond, or diamond-shaped.

encomendero. Holder of an *encomienda*.

encomienda. Grant of Indian labor or tribute to colonists by the Spanish crown.

entrada. Spanish military expedition of exploration or conquest.

ermita. 1. Hermitage. 2. Name given to barrio churches or chapels in colonial San Cristóbal.

espadaña. A pierced gable or arcaded belfry placed above the church facade.

estípite. A decorative column or pilaster, incorporating an inverted obelisk.

estofado. A decorative technique of painting and gilding for imitating rich clothing on Spanish colonial statuary.

fleur-de-lis. The lily flower, an emblem associated with the Dominican Order.

huipil. Traditional Maya woman's blouse, often richly embroidered.

INAH. Instituto Nacional de Antropología e Historia, a Mexican government agency charged with the documentation, restoration and maintenance of many historic monuments.

Ionic. One of the three classical orders of columns, distinguished by its voluted capital.

ladino. Chiapan or Guatemalan term for hispanized. people, usually of white or mixed race.

mendicant orders. Medieval religious orders committed to poverty and dedicated to teaching and preaching.

merlon. A decorative battlement, often pyramid-shaped.

milpa. Cornfield.

mudéjar. Hispano-Moorish architectural style and building methods; developed in southern Spain by Moorish artisans, or *mudéjars*, under Spanish rule.

New Spain. The colonial name for Mexico.

patronato real. Papal dispensation by which the Spanish monarchs were empowered to make ecclesiastical appointments in the New World.

pila. Basin or baptismal font.

pilaster. Flattened column used as an architectural element.

plateresque. Highly decorative style of 16th Spanish architecture, from *platero*, a silversmith.

portada. Main porch or entry to a church.

posa. Processional chapel, usually located in the church atrium.

pueblo de indios. Indian mission town in Chiapas.

retablo. Carved and painted wooden altarpiece.

retablo facade. Churchfront in the form of a retablo.

rustication. Decorative surface treatment of a building exterior in imitation of rough hewn stonework.

squinch. An arch placed diagonally across the corners of a rectangular building space to support a polygonal roof or vault.

Solomonic. Ornate column with spiral decoration, derived from the biblical description of the Temple of Solomon in Jerusalem.

tierra caliente. The hot tropical lowlands of southern Mexico.

Tuscan. Roman version of the Greek Doric classical order, featuring a plain column and simple ring or slab capital.

vecino. Spanish or white resident of a colonial Mexican town.

viga. Wooden roof beam.

villa. Official term for a Spanish colonial town.

visita. Church or mission without a resident priest, visited by the priest of a larger church or monastery.

zapata. Carved wooden beam-end.

INDEX

A

Aguacatenango, 73, 82–83
Alcantara, cross of, 40, 91
Alvarado, Pedro de, 13, 90
Alvarez de Toledo, Bishop, 43
Amatenango del Valle, 73, 80–81, 82
Americas, 15, 16, 23, 26
Andalusia, 21
Anne, St., 47, 79
Antigua, Guatemala, 43; architecture
    of, 21, 47
  Cathedral, 29, 32
  La Merced, 39
Aquespala, 89, 98
Ara, Fray Domingo de, 86
Archangel Michael, 30, 94. *See also* Michael,
    St.
Atlantean figures, 76
Aubry, Andrés, 75
Augustine, St., 76
Augustinians, 14, 15, 37, 47
Aztecs, 12, 14, 99

B

Barrientos, Pedro de, 103
Berlin, Heinrich, 113
Bernal Díaz del Castillo, 12, 13, 65, 99
Black Legend, 15
Brief Account of the Destruction of the Indies, 15

C

Camino Real, 89, 90
Cancuc, 42
Carmelites, 37, 47
Casa de Montejo (Mérida), 36
Catherine of Alexandria, St., 40
Catherine of Siena, St., 40
Catholic church, 18, 19, 22
Chamula, 12, 25, 54, 65–67, 69
  rebellion of 1524, 65
  church of San Juan, 65
  church of San Sebastián, 65
Chamulas, 19
Chapultenango, 117
Charles V, Emperor, 14, 16

Chiapa de Corzo, 18, 20, 100–109
  basilica of Santo Domingo, 100, 103–106
  chapel of El Calvario, 105
  church of San Sebastián, 100, 106–109;
    festival of, 106
  fountain, 11, 20, 101–102, 112, 113
Chiapa de Indios, 17, 18, 99, 100, 109
Chiapan, 12, 13, 99
Chiapanecs, 12, 99, 100, 110
Chiapas, 7, 11, 28
  ancient Maya ruins of, 7
  Catholic church in, 7, 11, 14
  church towers of, 99, 111
  Dominicans in, 16, 18
  highlands of, 42
  insurgency in, 7
  Spanish Conquest of, 65
Chichonal volcano, 117
Chicoasén Dam, 110
Christ, monogram of, 52
Christ of Redemption, 55
Christ of the Dungeon. *See* El Señor del
    Sótano
Christopher, St., 14, 30, 32
Christ's Passion, 41, 57
Ciudad Real
    11, 13, 14, 16, 17, 22, 26, 37, 42, 54, 100
Clare, St., 50
Coapa, 89
Coapilla, 117
cofradías, 18, 70
Coixtlahuaca (Oaxaca), 65, 72
Columbus, Christopher, 16
Comitán, 18, 20, 72, 73, 90–92
  El Calvario, 92
  San Caralampio, 92
  San Sebastián, 92
  Santo Domingo, 73, 90–91, 93, 95, 97, 109
Conceptionist Order, 45
Coneta, 72, 89, 91, 93, 95–98
  church of San José, 73
Copainalá, 99, 102, 110–112
  church of San Miguel, 110
Copanaguastla, 11, 18, 36, 73, 84, 86–89, 95
Cortés, Hernán, 12, 14, 99
Counter Reformation, 22, 39

Cross of Alcantara, 105
Cruz, Fray Francisco de la, 86
Cruz, Fray Pedro de la, 37, 67
Cuba, 16
Cuchamatanes Mountains, 93
Cuilapan (Oaxaca), 88, 103, 106, 109

D

Daniel, the prophet, 40
Descent from the Cross, 105
Dismas, 55
Dominic, St. 30, 40
Dominican architecture, 21, 41, 88, 115
Dominican popes, 41
Dominicans, 8, 14, 15, 18, 37, 64, 86, 100,
Dulce Nombre de Jesus, festival of, 57

E

El Perdón, retablo of, 52
El Recinto, 26, 37, 48, 53, 54
El Señor del Sótano, 43
Escuintenango, 89
Espíritu Santo (Veracruz), 12
Esquipulas, El Señor de, 61
Estrada, Alonso de, 13

F

Figueroa, Nicolás, 61
Flemish style, 84; Mannerist, 79
Flores, Carlos, 30, 61
Four Evangelists, 30
Francis Borgia, St. 79
Francis of Assisi, St., 30, 50, 80
    life of, 81
Francis Xavier, St., 79
Franciscans, 14, 15, 48, 50, 54, 59

G

Gage, Thomas, 26, 59, 75, 87
Gestas, 55
God the Father, 41, 55, 93
Grijalva River, 12, 14, 73, 82, 86, 93, 99, 117
    valley of, 73, 89, 110
Guatemala, 11, 13, 15, 16, 22, 42, 73, 89, 90
    artistic style of, 32, 47, 50, 57
    Audiencia of, 27
    Captaincy–General of, 11
Gulf of Mexico, 12
Guzmán, Juan Enríquez de, 13

H

Hapsburgs, 40; imperial eagle of, 53
Honduras, 7
Hill of the Nine Stars (Comitán), 92
Holy Name of Jesus, Franciscan province
    of, 48
Holy Sacrament, relief of, 40
Holy Spirit, 55, 93
Holy Trinity, reliefs of, 41, 79; altar of, 93
Hueyzacatlán, 12, 13, 26
Huistán, 13, 25, 64, 68–69
    church of San Miguel, 69
Hyacinth of Poland, St. (San Jacinto), 39, 72

I

Ignatius Loyola, St., 76
Islamic tradition, 102
Ixtapa, 12

J

Jericho, 86
Jesuits, 37, 50
    in New World, 50
    in San Cristóbal, 76
John the Baptist, St. 67
Jovel Valley, 26
juaninos. See St. John, Order of

L

La Candelaria, image of, 88
La Generala, 43. See also Our Lady of Charity
La Casa de la Sirena, 27, 35–36
La Encarnación, 45. See also San Cristóbal, El
    Carmen
La Quinta, 27, 62–63
La Trinitaria, 73, 93–94
Lacandón region, 12, 14
Las Casas, Bartolomé de, 8, 11,
    15, 16, 18, 28, 34, 37, 100, 103
León, Rodrigo de, 101, 113
Los Altos, 25, 64
Los Llanos, 13, 73, 90
Los Zendales, 67, 72

M

Marín, Luis, 12
Markman, Sidney, 8
Marroquín, Bishop Francisco, 37

Maya, 7, 11, 16, 20, 64
Maya Missions, 7, 22
Mazariegos, Diego de, 13, 26, 90, 100
Mendicant Orders, 20, 30, 76
Mercedarians, 16, 37, 53
Mérida (Yucatán), 36
Mexican Revolution, 19
Mexico, 100; Dominican architecture in, 115;
    plateresque style in, 21; Valley of, 15
Mexico City, 13
Michael, St., 67, 69, 112
Mixteca Alta, 115
Mixtecs, 26, 54
Moctezuma, Bishop Vital de, 50, 63
Montejo, Francisco de, 14, 36
Moors, 14
Morelos, state of, 15
Moses, 30
Museo de Los Altos, 41, 45

N

Nativity, 50, 79, 81
New Laws, 16, 17
New Mexico, 63
New Spain, 11, 13, 15, 103
New World, 15, 16, 21
    Catholicism in, 39
Nicaragua, 16
Nicholas of Tolentino, St., 47
Niño Atocha, 40
Nuñez de la Vega, Bishop, 30, 34, 39, 52

O

Oaxaca, 15, 18, 54, 65, 72, 88, 106, 115
    Dominican monasteries of, 88
    La Soledad, basilica of, 39
Oaxtepec (Morelos), 88, 117
Ocosingo, 64, 67, 69, 72
    church of San Jacinto, 18, 72
Olivera Ponce de León, Don Sebastián de, 79
Order of Friars Minor, 48. *See also*
    Franciscans
Order of Preachers, 39. *See also* Dominicans
Ostuacán, 117
Our Lady of Charity, 43
Our Lady of Forgiveness, 32
Our Lady of the Annunciation, 28
Oxchuc, 22, 25, 64, 67, 69–71, 75
    church of Santo Tomás, 69

P

Palenque, 7, 67, 72, 95
Pamplona, Fray Antonio de, 113
Pan-American Highway
    59, 73, 80, 82, 89, 93
Panama, 16
Patronato Real, 14
Paul, St., 30, 89
Peje de Oro, 57. *See also* Cuxtitali Bridge
Peru, 63
Peter Martyr, St., 39
Peter, St., 89
Ponce, Alonso, 102
Porres, Diego de, 43
Portocarrero, Pedro de, 13, 90
Protector of the Indians, 8, 15. *See also* Las
    Casas, Bartolomé de
Puebla, 15

Q

Quechula, 110; Dominican church at, 117
Quiché Maya, 26, 54, 57

R

Red Lord, 75. *See also* Votan
Remesal, Antonio de, 17, 103
Resurrection, 79
Rio Amarillo, 57
Rose of Lima, St., 40
Ruíz Garcia, Bishop Samuel, 19

S

Sacred Heart of Jesus, 52
Salamanca, 16; University of, 15; San
    Esteban de, 16, 21, 63

San Cristóbal de Las Casas,
    13, 16, 25, 26, 27, 54; Dominicans
    in, 40; religious orders in, 37
    Casa de Mazariegos, 36
    Casa de Cultura, 45
    Cathedral, 23, 27, 52, 63, 91; altarpieces,
        of San José, 32, 52, 76; of El Perdón, 32;
        of Los Reyes, 32; archive, 34; fa-
        cade, 51
    Cuxtitali, 27, 54, 56–57; Bridge of, 57
    El Calvario, 27, 55

El Carmen, 27, 37, 45–48; Altarpiece of the Virgin, 47; chapel of, 47; El Arco, 45; tower, 105
El Cerrillo church, 54, 61
Guadalupe chapel, 61
Hotel Santa Clara, 36
La Alameda, 43
La Caridad, 27, 37, 42–45
La Casona, 45
La Merced, 27, 37, 53, 55
Mexicanos chapel, 54, 61
Parque Central, 27
San Agustín, 30, 32, 37, 50–52, 76
San Antonio, 54, 61
San Cristóbal, chapel of, 61
San Diego, chapel of, 27, 54, 58–59; folk image of, 59
San Francisco, 23, 27, 37, 48–50
San Juan de Dios, hospital of, 43
San Martín, altarpieces of, 45, 63
San Nicolás, 27, 29, 37; La Encarnación, cofradía of, 34
San Sebastián, chapel of, 45
Santa Lucía, temple of, 61
Santo Domingo, 17, 20, 21, 23, 27, 37–41, 52, 57, 69, 73; facade, 30; priory of, 48; retablos of, 52; Rosary Chapel, 41

San Felipe Ecatepec, 27, 59–61
San Gregorio river, 98
San Nicolás de los Morenos, 33. See also San Cristobal: San Nicolás
San Sebastián, festival of, 75; statues of, 47, 57, 79, 106, 108–9
San Vicente de Chiapa y Guatemala, Dominican Province of, 17, 40
Sandoval, Bishop Juan de Zapata, 34
Santiago Matamoros, 30, 41, 45, 82
Satan, 94
Sayula, 117
Sebastian, St., 106; See also San Sebastián
Sierra Madre, 12
Society of Jesus, 79; See also Jesuits
Socoltenango, 88
Soconusco, 12, 14
South America, 63
Soyatitán, 73, 82, 84–85, 88; church of Asunción, 84
Spain, 21, 48, 99, 102; Church in, 14, 15

Crown of, 14, 17
Moors in, 21
Reconquest of, 14
Spanish Conquest of Mexico, 7
Spanish Inquisition, 14
Spiritual Conquest, 14, 17, 30, 40, 70
St. John, Order of hospitallers of, 37, 43
Stephens, John Lloyd, 72, 90, 93, 95
Sumidero Canyon, 12, 99, 110

T

Tabasco, 42
Tapalapa, 110, 117
Tapilula, 117
Tecpatán, 11, 18, 20, 21, 88, 99, 102, 110, 113–117; tower at, 112
Teopisca, 20, 32, 52, 73, 74–79, 82, 91; open chapel at, 22; retablos of, 23, 73; church of San Agustín, festival of, 75; chapel of San Sebastián, 79

Teposcolula, 115
Thomas, St., 71
Thomas Aquinas, St., 40
Tlacacaliliztli, 106
Tlaxcalans, 26, 54
Tlaxiaco (Oaxaca) 65
Toniná, 7, 72
Torre, Fray Tomás de la, 17, 103
Tovilla, Andrés de la, 36, 86
Tumbalá, 70
Tuxtla Gutiérrez, 13, 27, 100, 110
Tzeltal, 67, 80, 86; Tzeltal Maya, 69, 72
Tzotzil, 12, 69

U

University of Chiapas Law School, 50
Usumacinta River, 117

V

Vargas y Rivera, Bishop, 63
Villa Real de Chiapa, 13, 26, 100
Villalba, Fray Alonso de, 110
Vincent Ferrer, St., 40. See also San Vicente
Virgen del Rosario, 88
Virgin of Guadalupe, chapel of, 107
Virgin of Sorrows, 52, 55
Virgin of the Annunciation, 14, 30

Virgin of the Apocalypse (La Purísima), 30
Virgin of the Rosary, 41, 76. *See also* Virgen
    del Rosario
Votan, Mayan god/hero, 75

Y

Yanhuitlan, 106, 115
Yucatán, 7, 14, 21, 36

Z

Zapaluta, 93. *See also* La Trinitaria
Zapotecs, 54, 59
Zinacantán, 12, 17, 25, 54, 64
Zoque country, 12, 110, 117
Zoques, 12, 18, 99, 100, 110, 113
    chieftains, 12

MORE MAYA MISSIONS is the third in our series of illustrated guides to the colonial buildings of Mexico. The others are MAYA MISSIONS, in which we explore the churches and missions of Yucatán, and MEXICO'S FORTRESS MONASTERIES, which describes the 16th century monasteries of central Mexico and Oaxaca.

We welcome your comments and inquiries.

Additional copies of our guides are available direct from Espadaña Press, PO Box 31067, Santa Barbara, CA 93130.

MAYA MISSIONS	$12.95	(ISBN: 9620811-0-8)
MEXICO'S FORTRESS MONASTERIES	$19.95	(ISBN: 9620811-1-6)
MORE MAYA MISSIONS	$12.95	(ISBN: 9620811-2-4)